Critical Accl

"For Gershwin interpret⋯
— *American Record Guide*

"It just proves that talent always prevails in these times of mediocrity. Consummate musicianship."
— *Michael Feinstein*

"George Gershwin would have joined the audience in the standing ovation at the conclusion of 'Rhapsody in Blue.'"
— *The Hartford Courant (CT)*

"His fabulous encore with plenty of scintillating, puckish fingerwork on the ivories."
— *The Straits Times, Singapore*

"Bisaccia's performance of Gershwin couldn't be righter. It is all good fun and good music."
— *Edward Jablonski, eminent Gershwin scholar and biographer*

"A magical evening which just got better and better... completely passionate in his performance."
— *The Barrie Examiner, Ontario*

"Delivered with power, poignancy, authority and aplomb."
— *Worcester Telegram Gazette (MA)*

"Bisaccia brought the audience to their feet with genuine spontaneous cheers erupting out of sheer joy."
— *Steinway Society of the Bay Area (CA)*

"You really must hear him!"
— *Brasilia, Super Radio FM, Brazil*

"Earnest vivacity and sparkling virtuosity... infectious excitement."
— *Union-News, Springfield (MA)*

"A marvelous pianist who also enjoys being a showman."
— *Tribune-Review, Pittsburgh (PA)*

"Prepare to be dazzled!"
— *OnCenter Arts Quarterly, Hilton Head (SC)*

To Nancy,

Best warm musical wishes

4/4/24

PIANO PLAYER

Memoir and Master Class

Paul Bisaccia

PAUL BISACCIA

Copyright 2013 by Paul Bisaccia
All rights reserved.

Portions of this book first appeared as *"I Love a Piano"* in The Hartford Courant's *Northeast Magazine.*

All photos from the collection of Paul Bisaccia unless otherwise noted.

ISBN: 9781619272842

Cover photo by Steve Laschever: *Bisaccia in his studio.*

Back cover photo by David Morse: *Bisaccia before the camera for his second PBS television show.*

This book is dedicated to my parents, Raymond and Mae Bisaccia, who always showed such loving support of my career as a musician.

To Tim Saternow with whom I've had such great adventures making art.

And finally, to Luiz de Moura Castro - my good friend and mentor.

Table of Contents

INTRODUCTION

"Create memories." - *Franz Liszt*
"Say Yes!" - *Liza Minnelli from 'Liza with a Z'*

The inspiration to create art is found living in the real world. Go out there, live life to the fullest, and create memories you can use. To sit for hours locked in a practice room, pounding out notes on a keyboard, is part of the process, but not the answer. The nineteenth century composer Robert Schumann wrote, "I am affected by everything that goes on in the world, and think it over all in my own way: politics, literature and people, and then I long to express my feelings and find an outlet for them in music."

This is my memoir. Some of my memories are significant, others ridiculous. I've included stories about my teachers, friends and colleagues, and my unlikely career path from a hotel song plugger to concert pianist. These crazy and serious life stories are what I use as inspiration for creating music at my own concerts. I want to create memories for others through my performances.

I love the Kander and Ebb song as quoted above. Liza Minnelli had it right. Say yes! Say yes to every opportunity to perform, every opportunity to teach and every opportunity to share your love of music. Say yes, even if it's as a rehearsal pianist for a musical, or a gig playing background music in a hotel lobby. Say yes to making recordings and filming yourself. Put yourself out there.

I have been performing before the public for almost fifty years and I find people remembering my performances going back decades. Sometimes these created memories take me by surprise. Recently, an elderly woman who heard me play many times, asked her daughter to call me with a special request. She had been diagnosed with brain cancer and had only a couple months to live. The daughter asked if I would come to her mother's home and play a concert in her living room. This would be a special last moment for her mom to savor. I was honored and deeply touched to be asked.

Van Cliburn often said we need the healing power of music more than ever, and we need musicians more than ever, giving live performances to uplift everyone. My own teacher, Luiz de Moura Castro, always cautioned against becoming jaded. "Never take for granted playing the piano beautifully, anywhere, for anyone," he often told us - even when playing for audiences at senior citizen centers and nursing homes when you are given the opportunity. For these events you must strive to play even better. Occasions such as these show how music has powerful regenerative and spiritual qualities.

Arthur Rubinstein put it another way: "There is a certain antenna, a certain secret thing which goes out and emanates from my emotion. There's a moment where I can hold an audience with one little note, and they will not breath because they wait for what happens next. Not always does it happen, but when it does happen, it is the great moment of our lives."

Go out into the world, find your personal inspiration, and create memories.

PREFACE

Leopold Stokowski, Edwin Fisher, Arturo Toscanini, Ignaz Jan Paderewski, Shura Cherkassky, Lili Kraus, Claudio Arrau, Mieczyslaw Horzowski, Raya Garbousova, Myra Hess, Alberto Ginastera, Rudolf Serkin and Francis Poulenc. I know many of my readers' eyes glaze over reading these names. Most of these musical masters of the early and mid-twentieth century are now forgotten by the public. They are all dead. For me, these artists are not really dead. They live every day as I practice and they are an indispensable part of my work at the piano. I will refer to them throughout this book. (All of these artists still exist on film and recordings. You can look them up on YouTube.)

To write this book, I have tried to emulate Stephen King's book, *On Writing - A Memoir of the Craft*. In his book, King managed to combine a memoir with a master class for writers. In this book I've combined a memoir with a master class for pianists. The result is a hybrid - part autobiography, part homage to my teachers, and part "true secrets revealed" of how I make music. The process of preparing a score for performance is mysterious to most people. My aim in the "master class" portions of the book is to show how pianists do what they do, in simple language.

Thanks to so many colleagues who have read the manuscript over and helped answer so many questions, including Bridget de Moura Castro, Ellen Tryba Chen, Christopher Robinson, Jon Shee, Nigel Coxe, Andrew Bisaccia, Dominic Gagliardo, Tim Saternow, Steve Gavron and Brian Lee.

Chapter One

I Love a Piano

I Love A Piano. I love a piano. I love to hear somebody play, upon a piano, a grand piano. It simply carries me away. I know a fine way, to treat a Steinway. I love to run my fingers o'er the keys, the ivories. And with the pedal, I love to meddle, when Paderewski comes my way. I'm so excited, when I'm invited, to hear the long-haired genius play. Well you can keep your fiddle, and your bow, give me a P-I-A-N-O, oh, oh. I love to stop right beside an upright, or a high-toned baby grand.

- Irving Berlin (1913)

What could Hartford, Connecticut offer a 20-something starving music student? When I was a piano major at the Hartt School in the winter of 1978, Hartford had a calamitous event. During an unusually heavy snowfall the brand new Hartford Civic Center roof collapsed. Luckily no one was hurt, but repairs to the Civic Center would take years. This was a disaster for downtown merchants, tourism and hotels. The Sheraton Hotel on Trumbull Street (now the Hilton Hotel) desperate for any reason to get people downtown, asked me if I would play the piano at their hotel restaurant. It was called *The Hartford Stage Café* and it was always populated with theater people, as well as many interesting hotel visitors. Everyone who visited Hartford stayed at this hotel, from the members of the New York Philharmonic and Pavarotti, to celebrities such as Angela Lansbury and Richard Thomas who would perform at the Hartford Stage Company across the street.

I tried to gauge my playing to accompany the atmosphere of

the evening. If it was a quiet evening, I wouldn't be afraid to play strictly classical music such as Beethoven Sonatas and music of Satie and Ravel. I played lots of Chopin as well. If it was a more raucous night, such as an American Airlines party night, I'd switch to top 40 and Broadway show tunes. Of course, I often played Gershwin's songs in his original piano arrangements. These pieces always fit any atmosphere. They create an elegant, sophisticated effect, and *Rhapsody in Blue* is always a crowd pleaser. I told the Sheraton I would perform there for a month, and if they still wanted me, I would stay. I ended up playing four hours per night, six nights a week, for three years. The money (thirty dollars per night) was great for a penniless music student. More importantly, I was skinny, always hungry, and was allowed to eat as much food as I wanted. Occasionally the lines to get into my little bistro went out the door and through the hotel lobby. (As I recall, this was due to a savvy hotel PR lady who got me some well-placed interviews in the local press, which helped make the place popular.) I couldn't believe my luck. I was getting paid to do what I love - play the piano - and I could play anything I wanted.

I moved into the Goodwin Building - now the Goodwin Hotel, recently shuttered - directly across the street from the Hartford Civic Center. The Goodwin was a Gilded Age wonder and the oldest apartment building in the nation. It was built as apartments for the rich in 1882, so it was even older than the Dakota in Manhattan, to which it was compared. In fact, the nickname of the Goodwin was *North Dakota*. There were high ceilings, grand hallways and fireplaces in almost every room in the building. J.P. Morgan was one of the original tenants. His walk-in bank vault is still there in his apartment.

Sheraton-Hartford Hotel
SHERATON HOTELS AND MOTOR INNS

EXECUTIVE OFFICE

TRUMBULL STREET AT
CIVIC CENTER PLAZA
HARTFORD, CONNECTICUT 06103
TELEPHONE (203) 728-5151

September 13, 1978

Mr. Paul Bisaccia
743 Brewer Street
East Hartford, CT 06118

Dear Mr. Bisaccia:

Effective today, we will increase your salary from
$30 per day to $35 per day, with the understanding that
we will review your performance and salary approximately
90 days from today.

I also wish to take this opportunity to express our
appreciation for the fine job that you are doing, and the
way you go about doing it.

Sincerely,

John M. Roberts
Vice President & General Manager

JMR/kjf
cc: Accounting

The life of a hotel song plugger.

The owner of the Goodwin, Sam Greenberg, enjoyed having artist types living in his building. Paul Weidner, then the director of the Hartford Stage Company lived there as well as many people connected to the ballet, symphony, and opera. Mr. Greenberg boasted, "There are more pianos per square inch in this apartment building, than any other apartment building in the nation." I moved my Steinway grand in immediately and felt right at home. It took all of three minutes to walk from my apartment to my gig at the Sheraton. It was the perfect set up.

The wreckage from the Civic Center roof collapse meant that lots of critters went scurrying to find a better place to live. While playing one night, out of the corner of my eye I thought I saw a mouse scurry under a patron's table. Could it have been an illusion? The next night I saw it again - no illusion. I told one of the busboys we had a problem. The following night I walked into the room particularly inspired and raring to go. With élan, I quickly pushed open the keyboard cover and started to play the beautiful *First Arabesque* by Debussy. I played without looking down at my hands or the keyboard. It's a better way to concentrate on the music. Thirty seconds into the music there is a delicate arpeggio, which I played, hand over hand. For the first time that evening I looked down at the keyboard, to gently play the last note of the phrase. Where my index finger was about to go was a delicately placed drop of ketchup. It must have been the busboys' little joke. Just above the red drop, so artfully placed against the beautiful white keys of the piano was a little brown tail. It wasn't ketchup and it wasn't a joke. Obviously the mouse had made its home in the piano, sleeping inside the closed keyboard cover. In my haste to open the keyboard the mouse tried to escape, but didn't quite make it. I was horrified at the sight. The busboys cleaned up the mess while I ran to the

men's room to wash my hands many times. That night, I took a
long break before my return to the keyboard.

*A benefit concert at the Goodwin Hotel (formerly the
Goodwin Building) in downtown Hartford with Tony Award
winner Harvey Fierstein.*

Raya Garbousova

Raya Garbousova, as glamorous as a 1930s film star.

One of the most colorful patrons of the Hartford Stage Café was the celebrated Russian cellist Raya Garbousova. Besides being a great cellist and a teacher at the Hartt School, I am told that she was, in her day (the Roaring Twenties) a great beauty. In the period right after the Russian Revolution, she played chamber music with Vladimir Horowitz. They toured the Soviet Union together and were referred to as "chocolate babies" because they were paid in chocolate instead of money. She seemed to have been friends with all the greats of the twentieth century. She was a close friend of Albert Einstein. She told me once, "I played chamber music with him, but I'm sorry to say he wasn't very good and was always a little bit out of tune, but he was a wonderful old man and we became very attached to each other." Einstein remained a devoted fan. He would place a box of chocolates, instead of flowers, on the stage at Garbousova's concerts. I'll bet that was his own reference to her "chocolate baby" days with Horowitz.

I often accompanied the students of Madame G. I spent many hours in her studio on the campus of the Hartt School where she was an inspiring teacher and a real genius of the cello. Her sound was distinctive and warm. She knew how to make the cello talk. I'm not the only one who swooned when Madame G. played her cello. Early in her performance career, Pablo Casals declared her, "The best cellist I have ever heard." That is some-thing.

She lived in Chicago and commuted twice per month to Hartford to teach her gifted students. When in Hartford, she lived at the Sheraton and often had her suppers at the Hartford Stage Café, so I ended up seeing her at the school during the day and at my piano gig at the hotel in the evening. She always asked the maître d' to seat her in a corner as far away from me as possible. I tried not to take it personally. "Darlink," she would explain in her thick Russian accent, "I adore to hear you play, but not after listening to ten hours of students." She would always make a fuss over me, prompting patrons of the hotel to ask if she was a movie star.

Everyone in the cello world was crazy about her. She introduced us to a young Yo-Yo Ma who made a special trip to

Hartford just to visit her. She and her compatriot, the Russian cellist and conductor Mistislav Rostropovich, played together at the Bushnell Memorial Hall in Hartford for a benefit concert. She made her grand entrance in an impressionistic chiffon gown. Holding her cello aloft she appeared to float across the stage as if on roller skates. She knew how to work a crowd.

A New York Philharmonic Review

The New York Philharmonic was in town to perform at the Bushnell Memorial Hall. All the music lovers in the area attended the sold out concerts. The musicians of the Philharmonic stayed at the Sheraton and many of them were grabbing a quick bite in the café when I started my gig at 6 PM. I talked shop in-between my sets with the musicians before they began their exodus to the Bushnell Hall for their concert. The next morning, the Hartford Courant had a review by James Sellars - a smart musician and composer who knew music inside and out. The end of his review was the most devastating I have ever read. The last line contained the fatal words, *"they played like pigs."* Wow. After that bombshell I couldn't wait to catch up with the guys in the Philharmonic, so I sauntered over to the Sheraton for a late breakfast hoping to find out what really happened. One of the Philharmonic violinists, sipping his morning coffee, asked me if I read the review. When I said yes he sheepishly told me, "We really did play like pigs." The Courant got deluged with letters from irate symphony patrons. The next day the Courant apologized for "an offensive word" that was used in the Philharmonic review.

The Hilton Hotel

In the early 1980s, I received a call from the rival Hilton Hotel which overlooked Bushnell Park (now demolished and turned into a parking lot). The New England Governor's Conference was meeting in Hartford and I was asked to play at a luncheon given for the governors and their wives. Connecticut's Governor Bill O'Neill was the host. John Sununu, governor of New Hampshire (and later to become the first president Bush's Chief of Staff) spent several minutes talking with me about classical music and he proved to be knowledgeable. The party was a big success from the Hilton's point of view, and the food and beverage director - a real classical music lover - decided to snatch me away from the Sheraton. His name was Willy Schumacher. With his delightful German accent and gentle manner he made me an offer I couldn't refuse. A new restaurant was opening in the Hilton Hotel called *Terrace on the Park*. I would be given a newly rebuilt Steinway grand piano surrounded by comfy sofas, coffee tables and potted palm trees. People would come over to the Steinway with their glasses of champagne and request everything from Chopin Etudes, Mozart Sonatas, and works of Liszt, to standards by Gershwin and Berlin, as well as the latest Broadway show tunes. I prided myself on being able to fulfill almost any request.

At that time, the Hilton became the place to stay in Hartford and we had a constant parade of celebrities. Gary Hart came to town stumping for the 1984 Democratic presidential nomination. His advance man was in the room just before the senator made his entrance. He told me the candidate was depressed - bad poll numbers and a breaking sex scandal - so could I play *You Gotta Have Heart* from *Damn Yankees*? I played it, but I don't think it helped much.

Rudolf Serkin came to Hartford in 1985 to play Beethoven's *Third Piano Concerto* with the Hartford Symphony. He was a guest at the Hilton and dined one evening at *Terrace on the Park*. It was an exceptionally quiet evening. There was no one there except Mr. Serkin and his dinner companion, the composer Donald Harris. I decided to play the whole set of Liszt *Consolations* plus several Chopin *Nocturnes*. I figured it was soft enough not to be intrusive or too offensive. Later Mr. Serkin came up to me smiling and said, "Very good, no compromise." I can only guess that he was grateful I played these pieces as real music and did not fake it. The next evening I heard him play the Beethoven concerto. Serkin insisted on two days of rehearsal with the Hartford Symphony before he would consent to performing in public. This extra rehearsal gave an added polish to the performance. He was in great shape pianistically at that time and I never will forget his opening scales. So full, noble, and with a gorgeous direct sound that filled the Bushnell Hall like nothing I had heard since Rubinstein played there in 1971. It was that special piano sound of an Old World master.

Sundays were special at the Hilton. A bountiful champagne brunch was offered starting at 11:00 AM. It was the best brunch in town. People would line up at the entrance door all hungry and anxious to get in. From my apartment at the Goodwin to the Hilton was a brisk walk of two minutes. I usually arrived at 10:59, made my way through the crowd of hungry patrons all lined up, and sat down at the piano waiting for the doors to fling open. As the first guest entered, I'd start in on Bach's *Italian Concerto*. I always liked the idea of playing Bach on Sunday morning, and the march-like music of the *Italian Concerto's* first movement was great for opening the doors wide and watching the patrons promenade in for a festive champagne brunch.

One Sunday, we had a brunch calamity. At the table where the omelets were made to order, one of the gas fired burners suddenly exploded with a bang. Mushrooms, onions, peppers and parmesan rained down on the entire restaurant. Patrons were covered in vegetables. I kept playing - didn't miss a beat. Later during my break I picked out pieces of sausage and spinach from inside my poor defenseless Steinway. The following week the chefs had new electric burners for the omelets.

By the mid-'80s, my career as a concert pianist began to take off and I did less and less of the club work. I did manage to keep my fingers in it by occasionally playing at Shenanigans, the fabulous '80s nightspot run by John Chapin. I played every Sunday night. On Monday nights the great swing jazz pianist Teddy Wilson played at Shenanigans. (Teddy was the pianist with the *Benny Goodman Trio*.) I can't help but marvel that my unlikely career path playing club dates was born out of the wreckage of the Hartford Civic Center roof collapse.

Bad Reviews

Whenever I play excerpts from Gershwin's operatic masterpiece *Porgy and Bess* in concert, I always mention how the critics were unkind to Gershwin. The New York Herald Tribune review said, "Harmonic anemia of the most pernicious sort ... trite, feeble and conventional." Virgil Thomson was the cruelest. His review stated, "Gershwin does not even know what an opera is." I think Virgil was jealous of George. Virgil Thomson never had the celebrity or success George Gershwin had and he resented Gershwin's genius. Composer Stephen Sondheim, in his book *Finishing the Hat*, lamented that, "...few noticed how subtly and elegantly written *(Porgy and Bess)* was, least of all the critics."

I've been lucky with my own reviews. I'm only aware of one bad one. (Warning: it is *really* bad.) The review came from a prestigious national magazine which will remain nameless. The magazine decided to review a new CD of mine. For some reason this reviewer didn't like me or my music because the memorable quote was, "Mr. Bisaccia does not have enough talent to play the piano for a church basement supper." Yikes! My manager was incensed. He immediately called up the magazine and demanded a retraction. The magazine refused, but the reviewer was fired from the magazine a couple months later. I've kept a copy of that review in my desk for all these years. In this business, everyone needs a sense of humor.

Making Too Much Noise

Concert pianists are always worried about annoying the neighbors. We always need to practice and the repetition can easily get on people's nerves. In my case, I've had (mostly) wonderful neighbors. On occasion I will even get a call from neighbors asking if I might open my windows - they want to hear me practice. On the other hand, I must admit there have been times when my music making caused trouble.

When I lived at the Goodwin Building in Hartford, I often rehearsed with the opera singer Karen de Bergh Robinson. She is the wife of Christopher Robinson, the piano restoration *guru* who actually rebuilt both my Steinways. Karen and I gave many concerts in the Hartford area and one of her specialties was the aria, *Chi il bel Sogno di Doretta* (Doretta's Beautiful Dream) from Puccini's *La Rondine*. About one minute and 50 seconds into the aria there is a high C. It is one of most moving and dramatic moments in music and sopranos love to sing it. As Karen sustained this exciting high note, we were suddenly shocked by what sounded like a cannon shot. I jumped up from the piano bench thinking Karen had exploded a glass with her high note. Then I thought it was an earthquake. No, it was someone assaulting my door and shouting, "Stop that damn noise you idiots." I opened the door (or what was left of it) to find Ted Parker, the esteemed music critic of the Hartford Courant wielding a garden hoe. He had been hacking at my door with all his might, while screaming at the top of his lungs like a mad man. Of course I was shaken. I guess I could forget about this critic giving me a good review any time soon.

Later, I got a call from Sam Greenberg - the owner of the building. He had heard the screaming and wanted me to come down to his office. Was I going to be evicted? Luckily, no. He told me that he loved my music and I could play any time I wanted. Furthermore, he told the music critic for the Hartford Courant that if he didn't like my music, he could move out. That was good news for my living situation, but not good news for my relationship with the Hartford Courant Arts Section.

Arthur Rubinstein also had stories about annoying the neighbors while playing the piano. He was a night owl, and after a concert and a late dinner he had guests come back to his hotel room. One of the guests, fearing the lateness of the hour, asked Rubinstein what time it was. Rubinstein replied, "Oh, this is one of the great features of this hotel. I always know what time it is." He went to the piano and played a few fortissimo chords. Suddenly there was a pounding sound on the wall and a voice from the room next door shouted, "Don't you know it's one o'clock in the morning!" Later, the hapless guest went to the hotel manager to complain in person about Mr. Rubinstein's piano playing. "Oh, your room is next to Rubinstein?" replied the hotel manager. "We will have to charge you double."

Michael Feinstein and Gershwin

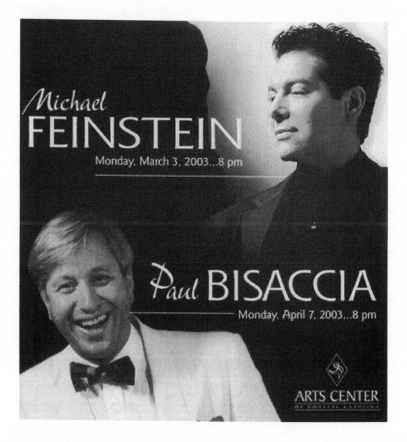

Michael Feinstein and me on the bill at the Arts Center of Coastal Carolina.

Gershwin's music was always a favorite of mine and I was the first artist to record all the solo piano music of Gershwin. The trick was to track down the music not yet published or otherwise unavailable. One bright summer day out on Cape Cod, I got a call from a couple music aficionados back in Hartford. Laura Holleran and Jan Grower were both experienced musicians and knowledgeable collectors of rare Gershwin music. They asked me if I would be interested in helping put together a concert and lecture of "unknown" Gershwin songs and solo piano pieces. I immediately said yes to their request. This concert would also be an opportunity to celebrate the publication of Jan's new book, *The Sheet Music of George Gershwin.*

Jan and Laura were also friends of Michael Feinstein and they asked his help in this endeavor. I became a friend of Michael's when I sent him copies of my PBS television shows. He sent me several letters saying he was a fan of my work. I was especially thrilled to get Michael's approval, because as a teenager he was Ira Gershwin's assistant. Michael helped identify and catalogue numerous pieces of sheet music and manuscripts for the Gershwin estate. I'm sure that his early experience, working with Ira, led to Michael's lifelong devotion to collecting and preserving old music, not to mention his legendary encyclopedic knowledge of the Gershwins.

Michael Feinstein became friends with Jan and Laura when Ira Gershwin asked Michael to contact them for a special project. Ira wished to obtain a rare score for his collection. The score in question was the out of print Percy Grainger two-piano *Fantasy on Porgy and Bess.* Jan and Laura had a copy of it. They made a copy for Ira. He insisted on paying them, but of course they wouldn't cash his check. His signature was worth more to them than the money. My good friend Nigel Coxe also had a copy of this exciting *Porgy and Bess* piano score in his library and I was lucky enough to perform this masterpiece with Nigel in concert back in 2000.

Getting back to Jan and Laura's concert idea, I immediately suggested that we ask Michael Feinstein if he could locate the unpublished manuscripts for two George Gershwin pieces I always wanted to study. One was *Ragging the Traumerei*; the other was *For Lily Pons*. These two pieces are bookends to Gershwin's musical output, composed at the beginning and end of his career. Michael was on tour and extremely busy. Who knew if he could locate these manuscripts or even find time to search for them? Both Laura and Jan said they'd ask him and see what happens. (I was way too shy to dare impose myself for such a special request.) One day, at a luncheon, I was presented with a surprise by Jan and Laura - copies of these two rare Gershwin scores. Michael Feinstein had come through. I've included below a little description of both these pieces. Even Gershwin scholars may be surprised at the unique insights these two small scores give us.

Ragging the Traumerei is George Gershwin's first known composition. It was written around 1912 or 1913. That puts Gershwin at about 14 years old. The existing piano part shows that even as a teenager, George had an instinctive and bravura way of playing the piano. The voice leading is very similar to Eubie Blake's ragtime works. Coincidentally, in 1911 Al Jolson premiered a song called *That Lovin' Traumerei* at the Winter Garden Theater. This song actually helped launch Jolson's career. In the following year Jolson recorded the song for RCA and it put him on the map. It wouldn't be out of the question to surmise that the Gershwin brothers heard Al Jolson perform this song live at the Winter Garden, and this gave George the idea to compose his own piano rag version. Jazzing up classical music was in fashion and Gershwin's "ragging" of the classical masterpiece by Robert Schumann cleverly incorporates the Schumann melody in both the verse and the chorus. ("Trau-merei" means reverie or dreaming. The original *Traumerei* from Schumann's piano collection *Scenes from Childhood* is a well-known piano piece. In the mid 20th century, Horowitz constantly performed it as his favorite encore.)

George Gershwin 1937. My first television show for PBS included Rhapsody in Blue.

A half decade later in 1919, Al Jolson catapulted himself into the realm of legend when he sang George Gershwin's *Swanee* (again at the Winter Garden) and at the same time made the young George Gershwin famous. *Swanee* was Gershwin's first big song hit and he made over $10,000 that year, just in the sale of the sheet music. My recording of Gershwin's *Ragging the Traumerei* was its premiere.

7/12/10   MICHAEL FEINSTEIN

Dear Paul—
Thanks so much for sending me your latest disc! It was so much fun to hear the realization of "Lily" as well as TRAUMEREI.
I enjoy your musicianship greatly, as well as your taste.
Enjoy P-Town!
Michael F.

Letter to me from Michael Feinstein regarding "For Lily Pons" and "Ragging the Traumerei."

18

For Lily Pons was found among George's papers at his death. Ira remembered that George wanted to write a piece for the French soprano Lily Pons and he believed this manuscript was that piece. It is a haunting nocturne with the flavor of late Debussy. When I say haunting, I really mean it. I was truly drawn to this piece and have played it for my own pleasure many times, late at night, with the light of a single candle. Gershwin was a serious composer who wrote music almost every day of his professional life. At the end of his life he was at the height of his creative powers. *For Lily Pons* gives us a glimpse into another side of Gershwin's art. He studied all the music of Debussy and he knew the Debussy *Preludes* completely. *Lily Pons* also has a hint of the Debussy *Cello Sonata*. The *Lily Pons* manuscript was incomplete, but I had my own special instinct on how to make it a complete piece. The conductor Michael Tilson-Thomas was a friend of the Gershwin family and he also had access to the manuscript. He recorded his own version in the late 1980s. While Mr. Tilson-Thomas was the first to record it, my version is different. It takes the music a step further and rounds out the piece to a satisfying whole.

As soon as the copies of the manuscripts arrived, I arranged to have both pieces recorded and included them on my CD *The Great American Piano Revisited*. I sent Michael Feinstein a copy of the new CD. He was kind enough to send me a letter expressing his joy upon hearing these previously neglected Gershwin gems.

Growing Up with Music

My great aunt Mamie, who lived in Falmouth on Cape Cod, played the piano in church and at the local movie theater in the twenties and thirties. Whenever I play ragtime like the *Spaghetti Rag*, or *Alexander's Ragtime Band*, I wonder how many pianists, like aunt Mamie, sat in darkened movie theaters pounding out music like this for silent films. My Swedish great grandmother (Aunt Mamie's mother) Annie Martinsen had a piano in the parlor. I was four years old when I first visited great grandma's farm house in East Douglas, Massachusetts. I remember the first time I saw a piano up close and it was this big old fashioned upright in the parlor. I was enchanted. How I wanted to touch those keys. I knew instantly I wanted to play the piano and that I would become a pianist. That is not unusual. Many musicians, from a young age, have an immediate and visceral reaction to their chosen instrument.

With my parents Raymond and Mae Bisaccia, after winning the Hartt Alumnus of the Year Award.

There was lots of love for music in my family. My mom played the piano and gave me my first lessons. My dad played the trumpet in high school and sang in the chorus. My great grandfather was a master clarinetist in Italy. He played in opera orchestras and was actually buried with his clarinet. My grandfather, Frank Bisaccia came to this country from Italy in 1903. Although a tailor by trade, he also loved music and played clarinet and mandolin. I still have fond memories of taking him to the opera at the ripe old age of eighty-eight. Poppy was very proud of my abilities at the piano, but I think he would have preferred me to become an opera conductor even more.

I have an old International *Cyclopedia of Music and Musicians*, published in 1939. In it, there is an entry for Giovanni Bisaccia. He was a successful opera composer, conductor and singing teacher. His teacher was the opera composer Donizetti. I'm sure Giovanni Bisaccia and I are related. Bisaccia is an uncommon name.

My earliest recollection of music was through recordings. I must have been about two when I figured out how to play a little portable record player. My music of choice was the greatest of all marches: Sousa's *The Stars and Stripes Forever.* I played it with the volume cranked up, starting at 5 AM. The only consolation I can offer for waking up the entire house, is the money I made years later on my own recording of it.

When I was in second grade, Andre Watts made his television debut with Leonard Bernstein on a *"Young People's Concert."* Those television concerts made such an impression on my generation and "Lenny" became a hero to us all. He singlehandedly inspired an entire generation of musicians. Andre Watts played the Liszt *First Piano Concerto* at age 16 with Bernstein and The New York Philharmonic. He became a sensation. His piano career was launched to great acclaim through Bernstein's mentorship. My dad bought the Columbia recording made by Watts and Bernstein and I immediately fell in love with the music. Even at that young age, the compositions

21

of Franz Liszt spoke directly to me. I was probably the only second grader in the United States to bring the Liszt *First Piano Concerto* in for "show and tell." The teacher kindly played an excerpt of my favorite recording for the entire class. Later, I taught myself the entire concerto on my own. I couldn't find a piano teacher who would help me with it. In college I won several competitions playing it, and there is still a film on YouTube of me as a student playing the big finale.

Chapter Two

Rubinstein

When I was young, my father took me to an event that changed my life - a concert by the pianist Arthur Rubinstein. This concert by Rubinstein was the first piano recital I ever attended. I look back on that fact as a magical omen. We sat right up in the front row. I had a clear view of everything. On this special evening I was given the template for what a real piano recital was, directly from the master himself, and I am forever grateful. This concert was a turning point, and set me on my path to becoming a musician. The second half of Rubinstein's concert was all Chopin. He played Chopin with nobility, poetry, finesse - a gorgeous sound - I was enraptured. Any pianist who plays Chopin must acknowledge the debt owed to Rubinstein. Harold C. Schonberg in his book *The Great Pianists* called him *the greatest living Chopinist.* I will always remember that night I first heard Rubinstein play the piano.

I heard Rubinstein again in 1976 at the Academy of Music in Philadelphia. The concert was a celebration of his 89th birthday and the 70th anniversary of his first performance in Philadelphia. When he first walked onto the stage he received an instant standing ovation. He did not even need to touch the piano - such was his personality. His simple appearance on stage was so powerful that his presence, by itself, was an overwhelming occurrence. Rubinstein was partially blind at this time, which made the pathos of the moment riveting. We knew this would be one of his last concerts. He played the Schumann *Carnival* - music that he had been playing since he was a teenager - with such poetic understanding and deep feeling that it was a life changing revelation. Recordings of Rubinstein cannot do justice to the sound that he created in a concert hall. It was so sweet. The sound fully enveloped and surrounded the entire audience. He also played the Chopin *Scherzo in B-flat minor*. When I filmed that same Chopin Scherzo for my television show, *Chopin by Bisaccia*, I mentioned my debt to Rubinstein on camera and how I thought of him, and this particular concert, every time I played this Chopin composition.

After Rubinstein finished his concert there was a surprise. A birthday cake in the shape of a grand piano - the size of a grand piano - was wheeled on stage to the sheer delight of Rubinstein and the audience. Rubinstein called out to the audience, "You see I love to have my cake and eat it too." The audience roared its approval. We were each given little boxes of cake to take home as keepsakes. After the concert we waited anxiously at the artist entrance to catch another glimpse of Rubinstein as he exited the hall. There was a limousine waiting to take him back to New York. Spontaneous applause erupted from the gathered crowd as he emerged from the hall. Still full of energy, and clearly touched by our tribute, he shook hands with everyone. I still have snapshots of Rubinstein shaking hands with a friend of mine, as well as pictures of the enormous cake rolled out on stage with a surprised Rubinstein looking on. We actually included these previously unreleased photos in my Chopin television show.

In 1960, Rubinstein wrote an article for *The New York Times* in honor of the 150th anniversary of Chopin's birth. In it, he said, "Chopin was a genius of universal appeal. His music conquers the most diverse audiences. When the first notes of Chopin sound through the concert hall there is a happy sigh of recognition. All over the world men and women know his music. They love it. They are moved by it. Even in this abstract atomic age where emotion is unfashionable Chopin endures. His music is the universal language of human communication. When I play Chopin I know I speak directly to the hearts of people!" My own teacher, Luiz de Moura Castro, said it even more succinctly: "I find Chopin indispensable."

Rubinstein about to return to New York after his concert at the Academy of Music in Philadelphia.

A Decision to Go into Music

I wanted to be a scientist. I was contemplating oceanography or marine biology. But the arts often have a mysterious way of interjecting themselves. During my junior year of high school I had the flu. I spent several days in bed just as a catalogue of musical studies arrived in the mail from the Hartt School at the University of Hartford. I read the catalog through and found that I wanted desperately to take every course listed - theory, ear training, conducting, keyboard improvisation, music history. I wanted it all. The three days I spent in bed provided me with the revelation to my life's work. It wasn't the flu I was infected with, it was the music bug and I've never recovered. I'm still enamored of the piano after all these years. Just looking at a Steinway Grand gives me shivers. Its sleek contours, shiny keyboard, massive golden harp and elegant logo still move me.

I told my parents about my plans to go into music and they were supportive. My dad gave me some great advice: "If this is what you want, you need to really go for it. Go at it hammer and tong." That saying stayed with me and I took the advice to heart. I give the same advice to my students. I was lucky to have supportive parents. Through the years I have known parents who did not support their child's career in the arts. That can be debilitating. Confidence is everything in this business.

My high school guidance counselor tried desperately to talk me out of a career in music. He practically screamed at me in despair, "You'll never make a living - it's a big mistake." Luckily I was not intimidated by him. (Maybe the fact that I was already making a living as a working musician gave me the confidence to disregard his advice.) This was the first time I realized that adults in positions of power can make mistakes. I'm still shocked by his bad advice. That experience taught me to tread with great care when I give advice to my students. No one knows entirely what the secret talents of an individual might be. Sometimes we have insights and intuition. That is all we have.

Giving career advice is a serious proposition. Choosing a path in music requires listening carefully to your inner voice. Everyone's path is different. Here's a quotation from Sigmund Freud that sums it up: "When making a decision of minor importance, I have always found it advantageous to consider all the pros and cons. In vital matters, however, such as the choice of a mate or a profession, the decision should come from the unconscious, from somewhere within ourselves. In the important decisions of personal life, we should be governed, I think, by the deep inner needs of our nature."

The Art of Practicing

High school students often come to me for advice. They enjoy playing the piano and get much personal pleasure from it. They are not sure what to do after high school and they come to me wide-eyed thinking how much fun it will be to have a career in music. It *is* fun, but you must be willing to sacrifice much. Music schools have practice rooms - all tiny and bleak, many with no windows. The pianos in them are usually awful. How many hours of your weekend are you willing to put into practicing? Sixteen? How about twenty? There are probably about ten geniuses born every century who don't need to practice that much. Unfortunately, most of us have to work at it. If you want to be a good musician, you must learn to love to practice. Many students find the grueling work too much for them and give up. If this work doesn't bring you happiness, don't do it. One needs to practice and juggle a real life at the same time. It's not easy.

Schools may prepare you for college, but very seldom is a student prepared for a career in the arts. If you do not think of yourself as a working musician when you enter your first year of music school, you may not be ready to start your college music education. By a working musician, I mean you should already be used to performing, whether with your high school band or orchestra, as well as in the pit band of your local high school musical. What about performances at your church or synagogue? Are you in a rock band, a wedding band? Have you already performed in a small concert setting such as at your local library or a retirement village? Do you go to concerts every chance you get?

In high school I was fortunate. We had a large high school with over 2,000 students. Music theory was offered as an elective. There were nine of us in the class and it met five days a week for an hour, just like a math class. This gave us a chance to do intensive drilling in music theory so it became like second nature to us. We loved it so much that we were allowed to have the class for a second year. Imagine two years of music theory in a public high school. The teacher who prepared our theory lessons was Stan Murzyn. He spent a good deal of time in the preparation of this course and I am grateful to him. I'm still in touch with my classmates from our high school theory class after all these years, because it meant so much to us.

The Hartt School, where I got my undergraduate degree, has about 500 free concerts a year. When I didn't have a gig, I was at a concert every night from my last year of high school throughout my college years. My first question to students who want a career in music is: How many concerts did you attend last month? I also ask them if they practice at least four hours a day. That is a minimum. There is no way to get through the mountains of repertoire without putting the time in.

I return to my high school in East Hartford, Connecticut circa 1980.

In my senior year of high school, I began studies with the head of the piano department at the Hartt School. His name was Raymond Hanson and as I write this he has just turned 92. He still plays the piano gorgeously. He has a natural approach to the keyboard, total relaxation and a deep sound - a real piano sound. He gets into the keys, as we say. He also has a funny way of saying things. He often had all his students in stitches. One day I played a very difficult passage from the Liszt *Sonata*. Played it note perfect. Then I followed with a simple little passage which I played poorly. His reaction - "You just tripped on a pin and killed yourself."

In October of 1972 there was a concerto competition at Hartt. The Greater Hartford Youth Orchestra was looking for soloists to perform. I got up my courage to ask Professor Hanson if I could enter the competition. I only had 6 lessons with him and he intimidated me. His response was, "I don't like to send people into auditions with ragged underwear. What exactly do you want to play?"

My sheepish answer was, "Beethoven's *First Piano Concerto*."

"So where's your music?"

"I thought you would say no, so I didn't bring it."

As he opened his mouth to express his displeasure I quickly added, "But I have it all memorized."

That soothed him. His studio had two grand pianos. I sat down and launched into the concerto. Mr. Hanson played the orchestra part on the second piano from memory which impressed me. I played the whole movement without wrong notes. So far so good. He didn't even stop me - very unusual. Professor Hanson's reaction at the end of the first movement: "At least I don't have to go through this music note by note with you." I think that was the closest I ever got to a compliment from him.

This competition became my obsession. I was determined to win. I refused to go to class for two days and instead spent all my time practicing. The fateful audition day arrived and I walked nervously into the auditorium. The jury asked if I had brought someone to play the orchestra part on the 2nd piano. I apologized that I hadn't, and one of the members of the jury said she'd play the second piano part. This was a lucky stroke. The judge was Anne Koscielny, a recent winner of the Kosciusko Chopin Piano Competition and a wonderful pianist.

Miss Koscielny smiled at me which put me immediately at ease. We played the first movement of the concerto and I dove into it with joy. I felt so lucky to be making music with such a wonderful musician - and me just a teenager. After the audition the jury told me to stick around. Then they called me back and asked me to play the concerto again. Wow - I'd love to. Anne Koscielny and I ran back up to the stage. We launched into the concerto a second time - oops, I forgot to give her the music. It didn't matter. She played the entire orchestra part from memory just like Raymond Hanson. Once I started performing, my love for the music and the thrill of playing with Ms. Koscielny helped dissolve away my nervousness.

A week later, a letter arrived announcing I was the winner of the competition. I jumped up and down like a seven year old. It was a dream come true. A few days after, I was back to Mr. Hanson for my piano lesson. He asked how the audition went. I said, almost apologetically, "I won." His response: "Well it's not that you're any good. It's just that there's no one better than you!"

More Beethoven Concerti

After the success I had with my work on the Beethoven *First Piano Concerto,* Mr. Hanson asked me to start right away on the Beethoven *Fourth Piano Concerto.* He wanted me to enter another competition. At that time I was far too young to tackle such a profound masterwork. That's all right. Working on something that is above your technical level can be a way to learn quickly. We had a good Steinway in the choir room at my high school and I would practice after school. As the janitors came around to empty the waste baskets I was still working on Beethoven. I would stay until there was no one else left in the school, sometimes as late as 9 PM. The high school gave me a key to lock up when I was done. I would turn out the lights and lock the music room door. I felt that I was taken seriously and trusted by my teachers. The opportunity that I was given to practice late at night would probably never happen today. In a world where lawyers have taken over the planet, imagine the liability of an unsupervised kid, late at night, on school property. Such things as liability didn't occur to us back in the early '70s. I think we had more freedom then. Certainly we had less supervision. Our time was less structured. Did this result in more freedom to create, dream and experiment? Perhaps.

Today there is a new type of freedom brought about by the internet. It changes how we book concerts and deal with managers, how we market our recordings and present ourselves to the world. Now we can download rare scores in seconds. Music that previously took years to locate with a graduate researcher crawling through dusty archives is now available at our fingertips. I use the web for research nearly every day. We can check out YouTube to see and hear historical performances by the great as well as obscure musicians. We can Google biographical information that was previously considered lost or unknown. A musician's web site can contain the sweeping history of an entire career - discography, bio, film clips and accomplishments. A musician no longer needs a record company. Just find a good piano, get some good mikes and a computer. Adjust the mikes just right and make your own recordings. Then sell them on the web yourself. Better yet, get in front of a camera and start producing your own videos. Thousands of people get to see and hear me on YouTube playing everything from *Rhapsody in Blue* to Chopin *Waltzes*. I often get engagements just on the basis of people seeing my YouTube clips. Presenters then call me or my manager via Facebook or my website. It's a new world and it will belong to the most creative, daring and clever.

I have owned all the rights to my recordings and many of my films from the very beginning. I know many musicians who have recording contracts with major labels, but have yet to receive a penny of income from all their hard work. I just heard the rebroadcast of a 1998 interview with the singer and pianist Ray Charles on NPR. He said essentially the same thing. It was shocking to him that most musicians did not own their own music. Charles said, with great pride, that he owned all his masters and made all his recordings in his home studio. I am pleased to say I managed the same feat.

My First Concert in Europe

I made my European debut in Romania, at age seventeen, playing Beethoven's *First Piano Concerto*. How I ended up in Romania will take some explanation: The cold war was at its height and President Richard Nixon was trying to diffuse it.

Nicolae Ceausescu was President of Romania. He was called a maverick back then - even though Romania was behind the iron curtain and a satellite of the Soviet Union. Ceausescu wanted to assert his independence as much as possible from the Soviet Union. Nixon and Secretary of State Henry Kissinger saw an opening and made overtures to him. Suddenly there appeared articles in *Parade Magazine* touting vacations on the Black Sea coast, and Romania as a travel destination for Americans. Most Americans never heard of Romania. A cultural exchange program was arranged by Romania and the U.S. State Department. The Greater Hartford Youth Orchestra was invited by Romania via our State Department for a three week tour, and I was invited to tour with the orchestra as the piano soloist. What an opportunity.

On tour in Romania at age 17. The Danube River and Yugoslav border are in the background.

We toured eight cities by bus. My impressions of Romania in 1973 were of a fairy tale world. We were transported back to the time of the Brothers Grimm. Little cottages with thatched roofs, large areas of dark thick woods, and beautiful mountains reminded me of something from another time. I expected Little Red Riding Hood or Rumpelstiltskin to show up at any moment. At many of our destinations, groups of native musicians, gypsy fiddlers and clarinetists serenaded us with virtuosic abandon. Up close, I heard the kind of Hungarian and Gypsy improvisation that Liszt and Bartok must have heard when they grew up in this mysterious land. Horses pulled wagons, and little old ladies with black dresses and head scarves sold goods from these wagons. It was a different world in a different time.

The people of Romania embraced us. One fellow actually rode his bike one hundred miles to hear me in two different cities. A little girl drew a picture of me performing in concert, and gave it to me as a gift. I still have this drawing framed on my wall.

We could see Yugoslavia across the Danube River and one night I decided to walk along the riverbank. It was shocking to see soldiers posted with machine guns along the river. At the Black Sea coast it was strange to look out over this vast expanse of water and see no boats of any kind. People could not escape by boat from the Iron Curtain. This was what life was really like in these repressed Soviet satellites.

My roommate on this tour was Alex Kuzma. His parents were immigrants from Ukraine, but Alex was born in the U.S. He was proud of his Ukrainian heritage and went on to become an esteemed conductor of the Yale Russian Chorus. One day, our tour guide announced that, for fifty dollars American cash, anyone could hop on a plane and spend the day in Kiev. Of course our chaperones refused to let us go. We were under age, and such a trip was impossible without the permission of our parents. For Alex, having a chance to see his parents' homeland was too much to resist. So we both snuck out of our hotel and hopped on a plane. We flew on the Soviet airline Aeroflot. This particular airline is one of the oldest in the world, tracing its history back to 1923. The plane we flew in was so rickety (I was sure the floor had holes in it) that it probably dated back to 1923 too. We landed in Kiev. Our passports were immediately confiscated by the authorities. It was possible the Soviets may have considered my roommate, Alexander Boris Kuzma, to be a Soviet citizen. Luckily this didn't happen. We were minded by a Soviet tour guide. Escaping him was impossible. We toured museums and went through the purported *Great Gates of Kiev*. (I say purported because the original no longer exists.) All concert pianists love Modeste Mussorgsky's *Pictures at an Exhibition*. The finale of this work is called *The Great Gates of Kiev*. Every time I play *Pictures* I remember this trip to Kiev. A fine lunch of lemonade and sandwiches was prepared for us at the International Hotel. We were also informed of the glories of the Soviet system. Pamphlets on the superiority of the communist system were handed to us, translated from Russian into abysmal English. When we were ready to leave, our passports were returned to us and we flew back to the Black Sea Coast. We didn't get into too much trouble from our chaperones for sneaking off on this adventure, but when we arrived back in the states our parents were horrified.

It's Easy When You Know How

Every musician dreams of owning a decent instrument.

Chopin says that students must always practice on a good piano. For concert pianists the industry standard is a Steinway. I can't think of any pianists in my circle of colleagues who don't have at least one Steinway in their homes. Growing up, the piano we had at home was a Story and Clark spinet. It wasn't useable. In 1974 I was completing my first year of music school. The pianos in the practice rooms at school were Baldwins - old, clunky, nasal, nasty sounding Baldwins. I get a headache just thinking of those wretched instruments.

I was desperate to get a good piano of my own. I scoured the classifieds to see if there were any old Steinway Grands for sale. A doctor in Bloomfield was retiring and wanted to down size his home. He was selling his 1900 Steinway Model A. The piano was six feet long, mahogany, with scroll work on the arms. It needed some work, but was a solid instrument. The price was $1,800 - my life savings. I bought it.

My parents wanted to know where I was going to put this monstrous piano. We were a family of seven and there wasn't much room. I suggested the rec-room in the basement. I planned to move down there with the piano. My brothers were excited because this opened a new bedroom for them upstairs. My parents were not thrilled about my living in the basement. It was damp down there, but I managed to talk them into it.

The bigger problem was moving this instrument into the basement. I called Ace Piano Movers. Their motto was, "It's easy when you know how." They came to check out the job. I suggested taking out the stairs and lowering the piano through the basement bulkhead. They measured and agreed to this plan.

The piano movers arrived with the piano on a Monday morning. My brothers were at school and my parents were at work. I was left alone to supervise. The movers, who reminded me of Laurel and Hardy, told me they had measured wrong, and the piano wouldn't fit through the bulkhead. They had another plan. The piano would go through the kitchen and down the basement staircase. First they entered the kitchen to move the refrigerator. As they did, a pitcher of milk broke spilling milk all over my mom's kitchen floor. Then Laurel and Hardy got the piano stuck in the stairwell. The piano wouldn't budge. They tried to shove the piano and put a hole in the ceiling. They tried to force the piano and broke a stair. The piano still wouldn't budge. They announced their next strategy. Remove the stairs. As they did that, the piano tumbled into the basement with a deadly clang. They killed my piano!

Laurel and Hardy left the disaster area with their tails between their legs. The damage in scratches, dents, and broken ivories was over a thousand dollars. It's easy when you know how indeed.

There is a happy ending to this tale of piano moving mayhem. I found a great piano rebuilder, Chris Robinson. He restored my piano to its former glory. I will tell you more about him later.

Chapter Three

College Years and Raymond Hanson

One of the best aspects of lessons with Mr. Hanson was his constant demonstration for us. I had the chance to watch, and hear how he played, and let it sink in. His playing was beautiful, the sound creamy and rich, the phrasing simple, direct and honest. This was most helpful for getting the real sound of the piano in my ears. There is also a visual aspect of piano playing that is important to witness up close. To play the piano well, you must have all parts of your body relaxed. I could see this relaxation, as well as the way Mr. Hanson distributed the natural weight of his body as he played. One can be playing the most complicated music, but there must be an effortless distribution of weight with no physical tightness. When it is done correctly, it is as beautiful to watch as a ballet dancer. Mr. Hanson perfected this idea of relaxation. You could watch as his hands floated over the keyboard, constantly in motion with no stiffness or tension in arms, shoulders or torso. He always said that his turning point as a pianist came during a snow fall. The gentle fall of snowflakes was his inspiration for the creamy, floating sound he always produced at the piano. To get to hear a master pianist up close and often, helped set me in the right direction. Mr. Hanson played chamber music constantly including dozens of piano trios and all ten Beethoven Sonatas for violin and piano with the violinist Charles Treger. Standing over his shoulder to turn pages at these concerts helped to put in my ear what a great sound should be. Mr. Hanson also played concerts with the violinist Roman Totenberg. Nina Totenberg, the well-known NPR legal affairs correspondent is his daughter.

I actually had the Hartt recording studio make copies for me of Mr. Hanson's performances of the Brahms *B major Piano Trio*, and Beethoven *"Archduke" Trio* (with Renato Bonacini on violin. Bonacini played with the NBC Symphony under the conductor Arturo Toscanini.) I played these recordings over and over for years. To this day, these recordings remain my favorites of these masterworks. I also heard Mr. Hanson accompany tenor William Diard in a performance of Schumann's *Dichterliebe* Song Cycle. The cellist Raya Garbousova had tears streaming down her face as she listened to this performance. (Later she told the performers, "Thank you for making me so miserable!") I was lucky as a student to be surrounded by these top notch performers who were real working musicians. Their hundreds of performances, along with the performances I witnessed by Rubinstein and Horowitz, still influence me to this day.

The Hartt School music faculty were devoted to their students. They devised a most perfect and imaginative curriculum for us. In my opinion, the best way to really learn the piano repertoire is to take it in huge segments all at once. For instance, one semester we tackled the complete thirty-two Beethoven Piano Sonatas. Every student was assigned four Sonatas to perform from memory in concert. Then, every Monday night we would meet at the mansion formerly owned by Beatrice Fox Auerbach, the department store tycoon. Her home had a grand entrance, an elegant dining room and a grand piano in a spacious living room. Myron Schwager and Immanuel Wilheim, both history professors, would present a lecture on the music of the evening. After that, a sumptuous dinner would be generously prepared by Mr. Hanson and Ms. Koscielny. They paid for this dinner every week out of their own pockets, and we ate heartily. Did I mention Ms. Koscielny was and is an outstanding chef? Back then, the drinking age was 18 so we had wine with our meals. It was all so elegant, and we felt so mature. After dinner we would retire to the magnificent drawing room and one selected student would perform four Beethoven Sonatas. There were enough students for us to hear all 32 sonatas twice in a semester. The next year we did Liszt and Bach. I was permitted to play six Bach *Preludes and Fugues* and the Liszt *Sonata in B Minor*. I was in heaven. The year after that it was Mozart and Prokofiev. Next it was Schumann and Chopin. In this way everyone was concentrating on just one composer and we got to hear entire swaths of the piano repertoire as one big immersion. I don't know of any conservatory in the country that could come close to providing this type of unique training. This immersion made us musically literate quickly.

So many fine musicians were in this class and I'm sure it is some kind of record that so many people who studied with Hanson and Koscielny are still doing good things in music. To name just a few of the people in our class who are still actively pursuing music:

- Carol Hess, a celebrated musicologist, has written several award winning books including *Manuel de Falla and Modernism in Spain* and *Sacred Passions, The Life and Music of Manuel de Falla.*
- Robert Ashens is a conductor and pianist who has performed all over the world. He is artistic director and co-founder of Opera Oregon and has a home base in the San Francisco Bay area.
- Carol Rich, who founded the piano academy in Portland Oregon, and performs regularly with the Portland Symphony.
- Ellen Tryba Chen has taught piano all over the world. I

managed to catch up with her in Singapore. She is currently teaching in Saratoga, California where she has many devoted students.

Studying with Anne Koscielny

Anne Koscielny - a pianist who can always be counted on to bring excitement to the concert platform.

Anne Koscielny's performance of the Chopin *B minor Sonata* was volcanic and her Liszt playing was meticulous and colossal. The clarity and precision of her playing combined with a passionate intensity made for stupendous performances. Later I heard Anne play all the Beethoven Sonatas - and again we were

42

all astounded by her artistry. Every great pianist has something special to offer - a unique way of playing that no one else can duplicate. Ms. Koscielny had tension and excitement in her playing - we would be on the edge of our seats - combined with a musical clarity that was very unusual. Every note was a clean strike. Every sound was clear - no mussed trills, no chords unvoiced, no melodies that were unfocused. If you combine that kind of clarity with the temperament of a real performer, you've got a special talent. Check out her performances on YouTube. No wonder she won first place in the Kosciusko Chopin Piano Competition.

Broken Piano Strings

A Chopin student once had a lesson with the master. He played Chopin's own *Military Polonaise*, and in the heat of performance the student broke a string in Chopin's piano. The poor student was deeply embarrassed. Chopin replied, "Young man, if I had your strength and played this Polonaise the way it ought to be played, there wouldn't be a string left unbroken by the time I was finished."

The Hartt School halls rang with sounds of both music and laughter. Mr. Hanson was always out in the hallway telling his corny jokes. At the time, both Ms. Kosicelny and I were known for our fiery temperament at the piano. We both made the piano "cry uncle." Mr. Hanson once told me, "I'm not so sure we should put you and Anna together in the same room. There will be too big an explosion." Mr. Hanson's prediction came true. I had a lesson with Ms. Koscielny on the Liszt *First Piano Concerto*. There is a recitative section where the strings are playing tremolos and the piano declaims dramatically. Anne

43

Koscielny told me, "Don't be afraid to get angry at it!" Oh dear. I did what my teacher told me to do and in 30 seconds I snapped and broke nine strings on the poor piano. Inside the piano was a tangle of broken wires. Later, Mr. Hanson could be seen running through the venerable halls of the Hartt School with a clutch of broken piano wires in his hands screaming, "Look what this crazy guy did to my piano!"

Legend has it that in his younger days Mr. Hanson snapped quite a few strings himself. I remember him playing the *Grieg Piano Concerto* with the Hartt Symphony and the founder of the school, Moshe Paranov, conducting. At one point Dr. Paranov mentioned that the orchestra could play out because when Mr. Hanson played the big finale, " It could be heard all the way to Alaska." I also remember Mr. Hanson playing the Gershwin concerto's final movement with an incisive rhythm. Most pianists like to play the last movement as fast as possible, but Mr. Hanson played it with great rhythmic vitality, and not so fast that he couldn't dig in at the accents. I thought his interpretation was the most satisfying and I've never heard anyone else play it just that way. I've taken a cue from Mr. Hanson and tried always to play Gershwin with that same rhythmic vitality. If you listen to recordings of Gershwin himself, there is a rhythmic pulse to his playing that is as deep and profound as ocean waves. You literally get swept up by his rhythmic surge.

Moshe Paranov

Moshe Paranov was the founder of the Hartt School and a legendary figure in music for almost an entire century. He was born in 1895 to Russian immigrants and passed away in 1994 at the ripe old age of 98. He was active in music, conducting and teaching until the very end of his life. In my young days as a student I was anxious to seek out older musicians with great memories and here was someone who had a knowledge you couldn't find in the history books. Rubin Goldmark taught music composition to Paranov and Gershwin in New York City. Paranov remembers sitting next to George Gershwin as they both waited for their music lessons.

"Uncle Moshe" as we all called him, made his New York debut as a concert pianist at United Hall in 1920. That same year, he co-founded the Hartt School of Music in Hartford. He was of the old school of pianists dating back to the late 19th century. His way of pressing down keys had a fluidity that you could observe as he did it. That "swan dive" into the keyboard was such an old fashioned practice. Paranov also did what we call "breaking of the hands" - an expressive mannerism from the late 1800s. In it, the right hand never seems to play exactly with the left hand. It is a very sentimental, old fashioned way to play the piano. We seldom play that way today.

As a high school student, Paranov was determined to make music. He asked his principal if he could come late to school. From 6:00 AM to 10:00 AM he wanted to stay home and practice. The principal said no - Paranov had to arrive at school on time like everyone else. Paranov quit. He never received a high school diploma. Later in life he did receive an honorary doctorate from the Philadelphia Music Academy.

Paranov gave the first performances of piano music by Debussy in Hartford in the 1920s. Back then, he told me, it was difficult to play this new music in public because it was deemed too radical. Debussy was considered by many conservatives to be a "dirty" composer because of his use of harmonies that offended the older generation. (Rubinstein tells a similar story

45

of how, as a student, this music was forbidden to him for much the same reason.) Uncle Moshe told me that to get away with his performances of this new music he would follow his Debussy with compositions by Mozart. In those days you had to "take a musical bath of Mozart" to get rid of the "offensive" Debussy harmonies.

Hartt School founder Moshe Paranov.

Paranov met with the conductor Leopold Stokowski in the 1930s. You may remember Stokowski as the conductor and collaborator with Walt Disney in the movie *Fantasia*. (Everyone remembers Stokowski shaking Mickey Mouse's hand at the end of *The Sorcerer's Apprentice.*) Stokowski was in Hartford to conduct a concert and Moshe picked him up at the train station. As the train pulled out of the station there was the high pitched squeal of the wheels hitting the rails. Stokowski pulls aside Paranov and says, "Isn't that the most beautiful sound!" Gershwin made a similar comment to his biographer about hearing music in the sounds of the railroad.

Uncle Moshe was in his late seventies when I played for him. He was very generous with me and his door was always open. He never charged a penny for those lessons. Like my aunt Mamie, he played in silent movie houses at the turn of the century. I think of that when I play ragtime. Beginning in the 1930s, it was conducting that was to primarily occupy Paranov, when he was named music director at WTIC radio, a post he held for over a decade. In those days, larger radio stations like WTIC, had their own orchestras stocked by the finest classically trained musicians in the area. Dr. Paranov led the ensemble in hundreds of symphonic and pops programs, many of which were broadcast over a nationwide network hookup. In a moment of which he was especially proud, Paranov conducted, as he put it, "the first notes ever heard" at the Bushnell Memorial, at the dedication ceremonies for the hall in 1930. The music he conducted was Bach's *Break Forth O Beauteous Heavenly Light.*

Paranov was a real character in his old age. With a mane of white hair, trousers pulled up to his middle, a Sherlock Holmes style pipe and a gravelly voice reminiscent of Jimmy Durante, which he used with a staccato delivery, he became a beloved institution. He would say things like, "Listen to your Uncle Moshe! I don't care what your mother thinks of your talent; I want to know what Isaac Stern thinks of your talent." He'd point to someone out of the blue and say, "Play me the Chopin *G-minor Ballade*. If you can't play it, someone else will!" He was responsible for bringing people like Myra Hess, Isaac Stern, Anne Koscielny and Raya Garbousova to Hartt. He had a genius for recognizing and collecting outstanding musical talent and he was smart like a fox. Paranov's life and philosophy were an example of the creative national energy and ambition, unleashed as he came of age in the Roaring Twenties. His dynamism was the kind of energy that made the U.S. great in everything from the Space Program to the entertainment industry. For Uncle Moshe the work ethic was everything. There was nothing you couldn't do if you put your mind to it and got to work.

The Beatrice Fox Auerbach Mansion and the Governor's Mansion

There was a legendary department store in Hartford called G. Fox and Co. It was founded in the mid-1800s by Gerson Fox. Many people consider it the most successful department store in the country. My grandmother actually worked at Fox's in the children's clothing department in the 1960s and she remembers Mrs. Auerbach overseeing the operation of the store personally. My brother and I would take the bus in from East Hartford when we were just 10 or 11 years old. We would get hot fudge sundaes at the restaurant (for 25 cents.) Mrs. Auerbach was all over her father's store making sure everything was just so. She was such a powerful and formidable Hartford icon that (according to Hartford lore) when the interstate highway system was being created, she arranged that the two major highways in the state not be connected. Yes, you read that correctly. For years everyone was required to get off the highway, go past her department store and then enter the other portion of the highway. Huge traffic jams would result from this highway disconnection during rush hour. She had been long gone and her 12 story department store transformed into a community college when a connecting ramp costing millions linking the two highways was finally built.

Mrs. Auerbach generously donated her mansion to the University of Hartford. The views of Hartford from the hills of her Prospect St. home were glorious and, as I mentioned, we all played many concerts in her living room. After I graduated from Hartt, I was often called upon to entertain when celebrities were in town to receive honorary degrees or otherwise be feted by the University. I remember a dinner to honor William F. Buckley where I was asked to entertain. For this grand occasion the piano was in the living room while everyone was having dinner in the adjacent dining room. Discreet piano music would waft gently into the room next door. I knew one of Mr. Buckley's passions was J.S. Bach so I launched into the *Italian Concerto*. Mr. Buckley bounded into the room with a dinner jacket and carpet slippers. He and I talked Bach with enthusiasm, and I also played some of the *Well-Tempered Clavier* for him. I was quite pleased to have Mr. Buckley keep me company, but I wonder what the hosts of the dinner thought when their guest of honor spent more time with me at the living room piano, than with the other guests in the dining room.

Another grand event at the Auerbach home was a party for the author Tom Wolfe. He came in carrying a little hand bag that had printed on it *The Right Stuff* - a reference to his best-selling book. He also wore his trademark white suit as if to imitate Mark Twain and he cut quite a dapper image.

Four houses down from the Auerbach mansion was the Governor's mansion. I played for various guests there on many occasions. When Senator Bob Dole was running for President in 1996 he came to the Governor's mansion for a fundraiser and I was invited to entertain. I was asked by his staff if I was a Republican. I replied honestly that I was a liberal Democrat. They all seemed to be good sports about it. (There are few people in the arts who are Republicans.) I noticed that all the guests for this fundraiser were grey haired elderly gentlemen and I was the youngest guy in the room. There were no women, people of color or anyone under the age of fifty. I thought to myself, Senator Dole was not likely to win the election if his support was only from old white male millionaires and billionaires. He probably thought so too, because he engaged me in amiable conversation. He knew he had the old white guy vote locked up and needed to reach out to other constituencies. Later his staff released a photo of the two of us together at the piano.

Midnight in Paris and the Hartford Connection

I recently saw the Woody Allen movie *Midnight in Paris*. Kathy Bates played Gertrude Stein and Adrian Brody played Salvador Dali. There is a Hartford connection to both Stein and Dali. I loved the film's capture of the ambiance of the Twenties in Paris. Many Americans traveled to Paris to take in the zeitgeist of the moment including composers such as Gershwin, Copland and Virgil Thomson. What does this movie have to do with Hartford? The oldest art museum in the country is Hartford's Wadsworth Atheneum. The director of the museum, A. Everett "Chick" Austin, made a name for himself and Hartford in the twenties and thirties. He was known as the first modern museum director. Chick was also caught up in that world of Paris in the Twenties and he brought that world to Hartford. People such as Salvador Dali, Gershwin (who was a sensation when he visited Paris in 1926) and many others came to Hartford because of Chick Austin. The legendary Ballets Russes had its headquarters in Paris and when the company fell on hard times, Chick managed to acquire the props, set designs, costumes and collectibles, and helped the company survive. In Hartford's Wadsworth Atheneum to this day are stored rare Picasso set designs and priceless memorabilia connected to Debussy, Stravinsky, Nijinsky, Diaghilev and many more of the celebrated artists associated with the Ballet Russes and Paris at the beginning of the twentieth century.

Chick Austin also scored a coup with Gertrude Stein and composer Virgil Thomson. The premiere of the Thomson/Stein opera *Four Saints in Three Acts* was given in Hartford at the Wadsworth Atheneum in 1934. The opera's director was a young John Houseman. Houseman may be remembered as the intimidating Professor Kingsfield in the movie *The Paper Chase*, which made him a celebrity. He also ran the drama department at Juilliard and did some memorable commercials for the financial house of Smith Barney with the tag line "They earn it." The opera was a landmark for its time and many people from the New York music and art scene made the trek to Hartford for the world premiere.

At the 50th anniversary concert in 1984 commemorating the opera's premiere, the pianist Nigel Coxe opened the special event by playing solo piano *Portraits* by his friend Virgil Thomson. I was invited to entertain at the glittering party after the concert. In attendance were Virgil Thomson and John Houseman (as well as Gertrude Stein in spirit.) Both were no longer young, but both had a twinkle in their eyes and waxed nostalgic about their exciting younger years in Paris and their work in Hartford.

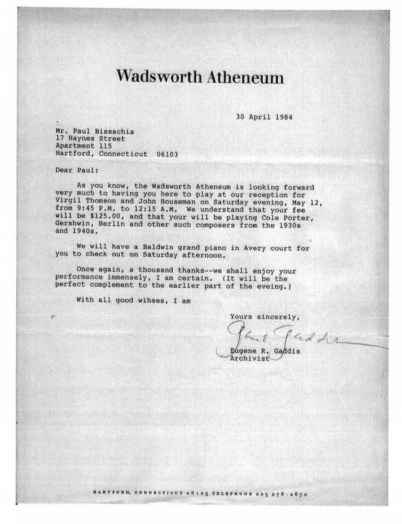

"Four Saints in Three Acts" Fiftieth Anniversary party for John Houseman and Virgil Thomson.

Chick Austin had a unique house on Scarborough Street in Hartford. It was known as the "Cardboard House" because while the length was of a normal house, the depth was only 18 feet making the house long but very thin. Chick fell in love with a similar house in Italy while on his honeymoon and decided to recreate this unique design in Hartford. Inside the house were exquisite and valuable tapestries, along with art deco furnishings. There was a small Steinway in the house and I enjoyed playing Gershwin's music on it because Gershwin was once a guest of Chick's in that very house. So was Salvador Dali. In 1994 the house became a National Historic Landmark and I played for the ceremonies officially creating the landmark status of the house.

I enjoyed playing many concerts at the Wadsworth Atheneum. One concert was a collaboration with New York violinist Paul Woodiel. Paul was a friend of Leonard Bernstein. During his student days at Harvard, Bernstein had written a sonata for piano and violin. (The style was very much after Aaron Copland. Bernstein was not only a conductor, but also a composer of works like *On the Town, West Side Story,* and *Mass.*) The sonata was not published, so Bernstein lent his original manuscript to Paul and suggested we play it at the Wadsworth Atheneum. I couldn't believe I was performing a concert off of Bernstein's valuable original manuscript. Here were Bernstein's own pencil markings and suggestions written out in his own hand. Paul Woodiel and I gave the first public performance together of the Bernstein *Sonata for Violin and Piano* at Hartford's Wadsworth Atheneum.

Playing the Piano at Mark Twain's Home

Before World War II, Hartford was known as the *Athens of the North*. Because of banking and insurance there was a good deal of money here and also a strong artistic and literary tradition that began with Mark Twain, Harriet Beecher Stowe and Wallace Stevens. Mark Twain's elegant Victorian home is around the corner from my Hartford residence. Twain said of his adopted home, "Of all the beautiful towns it has been my fortune to see, this is the chief... You do not know what beauty is if you have not been here." In the late nineteenth century, Hartford also had the highest per-capita income of any city in the United States.

Mark Twain wrote a letter that doesn't exactly bode well for us pianists performing at the Mark Twain House: "There's a damn piano player coming here tomorrow, and I'm upset because if there's anything I don't want in my house, it's a piano player." That piano player happened to be Ossip Gabrilowitsch, one of the great concert pianists of the late nineteenth century. Gabrilowitsch eventually married Twain's daughter. Twain seemed to have been pleased by the match.

I have entertained guests at the Mark Twain House many times. Playing Twain's piano in the late afternoon around Christmas time transported me to another era. The last rays of sunlight shone through the windows touching the ornaments and nineteenth century knick-knacks. It gave the room a warm, faded, sepia toned glow as I played the *A Minor Waltz* of Chopin. I felt as if Samuel Clemens would reappear. It was a sweet moment of reverie.

Chapter Four

How I met Luiz de Moura Castro

Taking a lesson with Luiz.

According to the author Deepak Chopra, "When the student is ready, the master will appear." This happened to me. One night, when I was entertaining at the Sheraton Hotel in downtown Hartford, Luiz de Moura Castro, the great Brazilian pianist appeared. He looked like a Latin Albert Einstein with wild jet black hair and kind, expressive eyes. Like Merlin the magician, he radiated power and command. He came over to me as I played and said, "That's all very good, but for you there must be more." Contained in his laconic statement was a crucial moment. I can't emphasize enough how vital a good piano teacher is to an aspiring concert pianist. If you are studying at Juilliard, Hartt, New England Conservatory or any number of colleges and conservatories, the number one issue is getting a private piano teacher who can truly help you. Nothing is more essential.

I always had the best teachers, and then I hit the jackpot with Luiz. He became my mentor and my friend. Luiz always had faith in my abilities and that changed the perception I had of myself.

Luiz is a working concert pianist. Some pianists who teach at colleges or universities don't have a real concert career. Consequently the nuts and bolts of preparing the score, and then actually walking out on a concert stage and performing it, is slightly foreign to them. Imagine studying to become a surgeon with a doctor who hadn't been in an operating room for decades. It wouldn't work. By contrast, Luiz is constantly playing most of the piano repertoire in concert halls all over the world. The advice you get from someone who has this type of practical experience is invaluable. To prove the point even further, Luiz was headlined in a book by Benjamin Saver titled *The Most Wanted Piano Teachers in the USA*.

A favorite pianist of mine, Garrick Ohlssohn, mentioned how much he loved studying with Claudio Arrau and it was for precisely this reason. Arrau was constantly performing and had the very practical advice that only someone who has played thousands of concerts can give.

Luiz, Ginastera and Advice from Composers

I knew Luiz was best friends with the Argentine composer Alberto Ginastera. I was working on Ginastera's *First Sonata* and it would be a real loss if I didn't play this composition for Luiz. This was the first piece I played for Luiz and he accepted me as his student on that day. He had much to tell me. Particularly with the Ginastera *Sonata*, I remember Luiz insisted on attention to the rhythmic impetus which goes from beginning to end. We talked about musical composition not just as isolated events, but as an organic whole. It is true that the great performances all have a musical line that travels from beginning to end. The one thing common to truly great performances is the organic unfolding of this line from first note to last.

A couple special stories Luiz told me about Ginastera: On Ginastera's death bed Luiz promised to record all of that great composer's piano music. Luiz kept that promise and indeed there is a two volume set of all the piano music of Ginastera recorded by Luiz de Moura Castro.

Luiz also spoke of preparing to perform some of Ginastera's music in public. He called on Ginastera at his home and asked if he could play some of this music for him personally. Ginastera said no. Luiz replied, "But Alberto, I want to know what you think of this music of yours I will be playing!" Ginastera said,

"Look Luiz, you are a fine musician. You may come to my house and if I am in a bad mood, or not thinking clearly, I may say something wrong. I would rather trust you to play the music in your own way and perhaps even better than I can envision. I do not wish to interfere." This was a wise composer.

In my own experience, composers are not only unhelpful to the performer, but get confused in analyzing their own music. The literature is filled with composers who felt their greatest music was a failure. Tchaikovsky thought his ballet *The Nut-cracker* was a disaster. Yet, it is one of the most beloved pieces of music ever written. Chopin thought his *Fantasie Impromptu* was a failure and ordered his student to destroy it. Luckily the student did not. Even if you do not recognize the title, you would recognize the immortal tune since it was taken by Tin Pan Alley and made into the pop hit, *"I'm Always Chasing Rainbows."*

What composers would think of our performances of their music is a complicated one. There is a story of a Viennese pianist, Marie Bigot, who was a good friend of Beethoven and Haydn. When Haydn first heard her, he embraced her and said, "My child, that is not my music, it is yours." She actually played Beethoven's *Appassionata Sonata* at sight from the manuscript for Beethoven himself. What a feat - and Beethoven had lousy penmanship! Beethoven's comment on her performance was, "That is not exactly the reading I should have given, but go on. If it is not exactly myself, it is something better." That just goes to show that many of the great composers would prefer inspiration and musicality over blind adherence to the score. There are stories of other pianists who made composers happy enough in their performances that the composers wisely chose not to interfere. Moritz Rosenthal became friends with Brahms and reportedly said to Charles Rosen, "Brahms never cared what I did." Debussy once told Paderewski, "It wasn't at all what I had in mind, but please don't change a note." Claudio Arrau in the book *Conversations with Arrau* said that some of the modern composers with whom he worked, "haven't known what tempos they actually wanted." I am always anxious to hear what composers have to say about their work, but like Arrau, I've found they aren't always sure what they want.

The Italian composer Arnold Franchetti was a student of Richard Strauss. Franchetti wrote a sonata for saxophone and piano for Brian Sparks - the principal sax player of the U.S. Coast Guard Band. I was asked to help with the world premiere. I actually sight-read the piano part from his hand-written manuscript with the composer present. I put the pedal down and faked my way through it with lots of energy and élan. I was inspired and the composer seemed not to notice all my wrong notes. He told me that because I was Italian, I understood him and he loved my performance. I was determined at the premiere to do the piece justice so I practiced it until I got every note perfect. After the concert Franchetti came back stage. He shocked me when he claimed he should have never written the piece - he thought it was a failure. My own feeling was that his music was wonderful, and I just didn't play it well enough. I had over-practiced and tried too hard. Sometimes wrong notes really are better. I felt bad for having disappointed this fine composer.

Luiz in Rio

Luiz was precocious as a young child. He was giving concerts at the age of 5 and made a spectacular debut at the Teatro

Municipal at the age of nine. He was doing mathematical proofs by the age of ten and as a teenager was correcting his teachers in his mathematical lessons. At age fourteen he won a national prize in history. By age sixteen he was invited to assist a mathematics professor at the local university. With his extraordinary gifts Luiz could have become a scientist, mathematician or philosopher. (You will meet more friends of mine later with this mathematical gift, which seems to be connected to music.) As a teenager, Luiz wrote music reviews for the largest newspapers in Rio. His city was a destination for all the world class musicians of that era and Luiz heard all the great performers from Maria Callas to Arthur Rubinstein. As a youngster, Luiz sang in a children's chorus that composer Heitor Villa-Lobos conducted. Later, Luiz would play that composer's music all over the world as the unofficial "Ambassador of Brazilian Music."

With Brazilian pianist Luiz de Moura Castro.

Luiz's formidable teaching abilities were apparent from the very beginning. Lili Kraus heard a student of Luiz's (who was not much younger than Luiz himself) play at a competition. Kraus was curious to find out who this gifted young piano teacher was. (Lili Kraus was born in Hungary in 1903 and like Luiz, attended the Franz Liszt Academy in Budapest. While on tour in Asia in 1940 she was interned in a concentration camp by the Japanese. She was released in 1943. During the 1966-1967 season, she performed 25 of Mozart's 27 concertos in New York City on a single series, and the next season played his complete keyboard sonatas. In 1968 she began teaching at Texas Christian University in Fort Worth.) Lili Kraus immediately invited Luiz to come up from Rio and join her on the faculty at Texas Christian University. Later, Luiz was invited on two occasions to become foreman of the jury for the International Van Cliburn Competition, also in Fort Worth.

Luiz's Musical Family Tree

Most important to me is Luiz's connection to the musical family tree of Liszt and Beethoven. Through Luiz I am connected to an important tradition and musical lineage that can be traced directly to Liszt, Beethoven and Haydn. Luiz's connection to Franz Liszt (and Beethoven) began in Rio de Janeiro when he was just a five year old child prodigy. He studied with Guilherme Fontainha who in turn was a student of Vianna da Motta. Da Motta was a Portuguese student of Liszt and editor of the first edition of the *Complete Works for the Piano* by Liszt. Luiz also studied at the Franz Liszt Academy in Budapest Hungary, which was founded by Liszt himself. In Budapest, he had private lessons with Joseph Gat, who was on the faculty of the Liszt Academy. Gat was a student of Isztvan Toman, another student of Liszt. The family musical tree goes back further - Liszt studied in Vienna with Carl Czerny. Carl Czerny was Beethoven's close friend and prized piano student. Czerny himself was also the most important piano teacher in Vienna at that time. Czerny actually arranged for Liszt to meet with Beethoven.

Franz Liszt in old age.

Liszt, in his old age, gave this oral account to his pupil Ilka Horowitz-Barnay of his meeting with Beethoven (taken here from part one of Alan Walker's superb three part biography of Liszt in which Walker quotes this story from the *Neue Freie Presse*, July 7, 1898.):

"I was about eleven years of age when my venerated teacher Czerny took me to Beethoven. He had told the latter about me a

long time before, and had begged him to listen to me play sometime. Yet Beethoven had such a repugnance to infant prodigies that he had always violently objected to receiving me. Finally, however he allowed himself to be persuaded by the indefatigable Czerny, and in the end cried impatiently: 'In God's name, then, bring me the young Turk!' It was ten o'clock in the morning when we entered the two small rooms in the Schwarzspanier house which Beethoven occupied, I somewhat shyly, Czerny amiably encouraging me. Beethoven was working at a long table by the window. He looked gloomily at us for a time, said a few brief words to Czerny, and remained silent when my kind teacher beckoned me to the piano. I played a short piece by Ries. When I finished, Beethoven asked me whether I could play a Bach Fugue. I chose the C-minor Fugue from the Well-Tempered Clavier. 'And could you also transpose the fugue at once into another key?' Beethoven asked me. Fortunately I was able to do so. After my closing chord I glanced up. The great master's darkly glowing gaze lay piercingly upon me. Yet suddenly a smile passed over his gloomy features, and Beethoven came quite close to me, stooped down, put his hand on my head and stroked my hair several times. 'A devil of a fellow,' he whispered, 'a regular young Turk!' Suddenly I felt quite brave. 'May I play something of yours now?' I boldly asked. Beethoven smiled and nodded. I played the first movement of the C-major Concerto. When I had concluded, Beethoven caught hold of me with both hands, kissed me on the forehead, and said gently: 'Go! You are one of the fortunate ones! For you will give joy and happiness to many other people! There is nothing better or finer!' Liszt told the preceding in a tone of deepest emotion, with tears in his eyes, and a warm note of happiness sounded in the simple tale. For a brief space he was silent, and then he said: "This event in my life has remained my greatest pride - the palladium of my whole career as an artist. I tell it but very seldom and - only to good friends!"

This tale is significant for the special relationship between Liszt and Beethoven. Liszt was one of the great interpreters of Beethoven's music in the nineteenth century and Liszt handed this Beethoven tradition down to his students who in turn handed it down to us. Liszt even acquired Beethoven's Broadwood piano and regarded it as a special icon.

Liszt was incredibly devoted to his students, and Luiz carries on the same devotion to his students to this day.

Liszt also founded the tradition of the master class. A master class is a gathering of all the students to perform. The teacher listens, criticizes and demonstrates for the benefit of all. It is a wonderful way to learn and the Liszt master classes have become legendary to piano students. Luiz has carried on that tradition taken directly from Liszt and I have seen many student performances transformed through Luiz's tutelage in these master classes.

We can even go further in the family tree: Beethoven's teacher was Haydn. Haydn was the Father of the Symphony and to a certain extent the Piano Sonata. When I teach a Haydn Sonata to one of my students, I often think of the mighty line of teachers I'm connected to, going directly back to Haydn.

Beethoven's patron, the young Count Waldstein, famously writes the following in November 1792 in Beethoven's personal album (just months after Mozart's tragic death) as Beethoven prepares to leave Bonn for Vienna and his greatly anticipated apprenticeship to his new teacher, Haydn. Here is the translation taken from Lewis Lockwood's book *The Music and the Life of Beethoven*:

"Dear Beethoven! You are going to Vienna in fulfillment of a wish that has long been frustrated. Mozart's genius is still in mourning and weeps for the death of its pupil. It found a refuge with the inexhaustible Haydn but no occupation; through him it wishes to form a union with another. With the help of unceasing diligence you will receive the spirit of Mozart from the hand of Haydn."

Wow! Even back then it was clear that this divine spark of musical inspiration was delicate and could only be transmitted from teacher to pupil with utmost care. Just to make this musical family tree clear: Haydn taught Beethoven. Beethoven taught Czerny. Czerny taught Liszt. Liszt taught Isztvan Toman. Isztvan Toman taught Joseph Gat. Joseph Gat taught Luiz de Moura Castro. Luiz de Moura Castro taught me. Here we see seven generations of musicians from the mid 1700s to the present. I can't stress enough how Luiz and I see that lineage as a direct connection to the very essence of what music means to us. Every day, as teachers and performers, Luiz and I are constantly reminded of our historic connection to these men of genius.

The 10,000 Hour Rule

The Holy Grail of piano study is finding the right teacher. The one-on-one work between a master teacher and an aspiring musician must be done slowly and with patience - and it works both ways. Teacher and pupil must both have patience. The Latin motto is *Festina lente* - "Make haste slowly." Like most crafts, a careful and thorough instruction is fundamental. Both Luiz and I agree on this: If you can apprentice with a master, to really get the hang of it all takes about seven years. In Malcolm

Gladwell's book *Outliers* he puts it a little differently. He says that to become a true master of anything you need to put in your 10,000 hours. He devotes an entire chapter to it called *The 10,000 Hour Rule*. Gladwell uses the example of the Beatles and their apprenticeship in Hamburg where they played night clubs for eight hours a night for 270 nights in just a year and a half. Beatles biographer Philip Norman is quoted as saying, "They learned not only stamina. They had to learn an enormous amount of numbers - cover versions of everything you can think of, not just rock and roll, a bit of jazz too. They weren't disciplined onstage at all before that. But when they came back, (to Britain) they sounded like no one else. It was the making of them." I can't help but think that in my own case, performing four hours per night, six nights per week for six years during my student years, was a great lesson for me in stamina and repertoire. Sometimes people ask me after a concert if I am tired. Just the opposite - I can play the whole concert again. I seldom get tired. This goes back to the discipline of playing for hours as a student.

Raymond Hanson and Anne Koscielny were the stars of the piano department at Hartt. During my last year as an undergraduate they invited Luiz to give master classes and a concert. Many performers/teachers are jealous of their colleagues, especially if they are good. It is just human nature. To their everlasting credit, Hanson and Koscielny could tell who was really good and were always interested in the best. They were such fine artists themselves, that they had the confidence to invite people with great talent. Luiz impressed everyone because he had a unique talent as a teacher to help students. He would whisper suggestions to one student, suggest a different hand position to another, invite a student to work at relaxation of the muscles so that the music could really flow. He did this in a gentle understated way that made it possible for the students to take in his suggestions quickly and thoroughly, almost as if the students were given a post-hypnotic suggestion. All of a sudden we were hearing authentic Beethoven, authentic Chopin, authentic Liszt. These were now living composers who spoke to us through their music. Luiz has a gift for this and he was hired immediately as a professor of piano at Hartt. As I write these words Luiz just celebrated his 70th birthday. He still teaches at Hartt where students come from all over Europe, Asia and South America to study with him.

Alan Walker Reviews Luiz in Concert

One of my heroes is the eminent Liszt expert Alan Walker. His formidable three volume biography of Liszt never leaves my bedside. It is one of my favorite books to read. Anyone who loves Liszt needs to read this book. The first volume alone took him 10 years to write. So much that has come down to us of the Liszt legend is filled with falsehoods. Dr. Walker in his research manages to finally get at the truth of this genius of the piano. In many areas of Liszt scholarship his books are really the first to set the record straight. These books have won the James Tait Black Award for best biography and the Medal of the Hungarian Minister of Culture. When Luiz gave an all Liszt recital in Eugene Oregon in the spring of 2012, Alan Walker wrote a wonderful review of the concert. A CD of the concert has been released and it is a favorite of mine. Dr. Walker has graciously allowed his review of that concert to be published here:

Those of us who were privileged to hear Luiz de Moura Castro's all-Liszt recital in Eugene the other day, witnessed some unforgettable piano playing. This was music-making of a kind that comes along but rarely. I have heard many Liszt recitals across the years, but can recall nothing quite like the one that Mr. de Moura Castro offered us on this occasion. Like some Merlin of the Piano he cast his spells across the keyboard, drew us into his charmed circle, and beguiled us with one magical effect after another. Here was piano playing from a Golden Age that most of us thought had vanished beyond recall.

Mr. de Moura Castro walks on stage very slowly and advances towards the keyboard as if he is reluctant to offer the bounty he has so lovingly prepared and is about to present to us. He settles himself at the keyboard gently, as if searching for the best point of repose, and he allows himself a moment's reflection before beginning to play. In fact, he does not play the piano as much as preside over it, coaxing it to do his bidding. And the piano complies, delighting in the fact that here, at last, is a musician who knows how to treat it well and draw the very best out of it. Mr. de Moura Castro's fingers remain in constant contact with the keys, until those 88 inanimate objects begin to murmur, then to sing, and finally rejoice in the knowledge that they are under the command of a master pianist. When was the last time we heard a genuine pianissimo in the concert hall? I do not wish to be misunderstood. It is not a question of playing softly. It is a question of knowing how to send that softness to the back of the hall. Mr. de Moura Castro's control of nuance is complete. And there is one more thing. He barely moves while he plays. Not for him the vulgar choreography of so many younger pianists who throw themselves all over the keyboard in a visible display of 'work', and the possibility of gaining some cheap applause. The quiet dignity of his demeanor invested his interpretations with authority, and proved the truth of the old adage, 'the less the more'.

There was nothing in the printed programme to suggest that anything unusual was about to happen. It seemed to be a conventional sort of recital, even a commonplace one, an occasion that one might happily forgo in favour of something more adventurous.

Six Consolations
Three Petrarch Sonnets
Funérailles (1849)

Then something extraordinary occurred, which I never before observed in the concert hall. At the close of the Six Consolations, and the long silence that ensued, the audience suddenly erupted and offered Mr. de Moura Castro a standing ovation. A standing ovation for the Six Consolations - the simplest and least virtu-osic pieces that Liszt ever penned! It was the first indication that we wished to say thank you to this pianist for drawing us into an inner world of beauty all too often absent in Liszt recitals, where the purpose seems to be to pound the piano through the floorboards.

It has been well said that inside every great pianist is a singer trying to get out. Mr. de Moura Castro's performance of the three Petrarch Sonnets was an object lesson in how to turn the piano into a sustaining instrument of radiant beauty. Liszt's melodies were boldly sculpted and made to stand out in sharp relief against their rich harmonic backgrounds. And they were phrased to perfection. Busoni's comments about 'the enthroned golden sound' came to mind, an image which seemed to hover over this recital like a benediction.

Finally came Funérailles (1849). We had already heard the

piano yield a generous palette of colours. But Mr. de Moura Castro now made the instrument lament, grieve, and finally exult in the course of Liszt's magnificent tribute to a Hungary in mourning after the national catastrophe of 1849. There is virtuosity aplenty in *Funérailles*. But the great virtue of this performance was that it simply disappeared in the service of the music. (The words 'virtuosity' and 'virtue' spring from the same root. Failure to attend to that fact lies at the heart of much inferior Liszt playing.) Even the famous left-hand octave passages towards the conclusion of the piece poured out of the instrument in an ever-growing torrent of sound, while the pianist remained virtually immobile. And the sound always remained rich and full. It brought the recital to a climactic end, garnered several curtain calls, and a general clamour for more.

So Mr. de Moura Castro generously obliged. He returned to the keyboard - not with a fleet-fingered display piece meant to astonish and impress, but with one of Mendelssohn's simple *Song Without Words* - the one in E major subtitled 'Sweet Remembrance'. Was the choice deliberate? Had the pianist begun to toy with us, commenting on his own recital? The thought was not entirely chimerical. Even before the final E-major chord had vanished, he moved straight into Mendelssohn's 'Spring Song' - a deliberately puckish interpretation which seemed to make light of everything that he had just accomplished.

Although words about music have been my *métier* for most of my professional life, I would require the pen of a Dickens or a Balzac to do justice in prose to this recital. Since I am neither a Dickens nor a Balzac, I must borrow from poetry and fall back on some lines from Wordsworth:

> "That music in my heart I bore,
> Long after it was heard no more"

Nigel Coxe

Nigel Coxe - a pianist with intellect and a beautiful old-fashioned sound.

Another favorite pianist of mine is Nigel Coxe. In his eighties and still actively performing, Nigel lives in Amherst, Massachusetts and has taught for years at the University of Massachusetts. I've had the pleasure of hearing him play in concert on many occasions. I love his playing. It's the old-fashioned kind with a truly beautiful sound - focused and pure.

He has a direct connection to the music he plays, and it unfolds with poetry and finesse. I remember when the Advocate Newspapers gave him an award for best concert of the year. Nigel won the important *Harold Samuel Bach Prize* in England on July 8th 1952 and the legendary pianist, Dame Myra Hess, presented him with that award. This was a real coup for Nigel. Myra was one of the most beloved pianists in England. She courageously played concerts during World War II under frightening circumstances, refusing to stop playing even in the midst of exploding bombs. There are film clips of her on YouTube performing Beethoven's *Appassionata* where she attacks the piece with fury. Her courage and talent made her one of the most beloved pianists of the 20th century and a national hero in Britain.

When he began his career, Nigel obtained an audition with the BBC. These were blind auditions where the auditioner played behind a screen. Nigel won the audition and in 1956 at age 24 he began broadcasting regularly with the BBC. He started performing in the 9 AM slot. This was where pianists started out. The truly coveted time slots were in the evening, and being asked to play in these evening time slots was a great honor. Eventually, because of his success, Nigel was invited to perform on these evening broadcasts. To master so much musical material so quickly for these radio appearances was a huge undertaking. This brings me yet again to the *10,000 Hour Rule*. Nigel credits his success with the hours of hard work he put in with the BBC.

In the previous chapter I mentioned the writer and Liszt Scholar Alan Walker, who wrote the enclosed review of my teacher Luiz's recent concert. I've also quoted from Dr. Walker's brilliant three volume book on Liszt. I fell off my chair when Nigel told me recently that the radio producer for his BBC concerts in London was none other than Alan Walker! Six degrees of separation really is only two degrees of separation in the music business.

As Nigel's success grew at the BBC, he was invited to perform in live broadcasts as a soloist with the famed Hallé Orchestra. The principal conductor of the Hallé was Sir John Barbirolli - one of Rubinstein's favorite conductors. For this concert Nigel was to perform Rachmaninoff's *Rhapsody on a Theme of Paganini* with the assistant conductor, George Weldon. Nigel had never played this piece. He asked if he could play a concerto he already knew instead. The powers that be said no, so Nigel had to learn this most difficult concerto in three weeks - quite a feat. First performances of works can be nerve-wracking. To add to the stress of this undertaking, the conductor went missing minutes before the broadcast. With no conductor in sight the first number on the program was conducted at the last minute by the concert master, Martin Milner. Nigel was next on the broadcast and just in time the conductor, Mr. Weldon, appeared with a bruise on his head. He had taken a serious fall just before the concert. As they walked out together, Nigel realized the conductor was unsteady. With the conductor's first down beat to the orchestra Nigel knew he was in trouble as Weldon swayed and almost lost his balance. Nigel and the concertmaster, terrified, watched each other carefully and tried to play without the conductor. After the broadcast Milner came to the artist room saying, "Nigel, you are a bloody hero! Thank goodness you knew this piece so well. You must have played it many times to play it so well under these impossible conditions." Miraculously, no one could tell that Nigel had so hastily learned the music and this was his first performance of it. Two weeks later Nigel was stunned to hear a radio news bulletin. The conductor George Weldon had suddenly died on tour in South Africa.

Nigel, like Luiz, was a pupil of a pupil of Liszt. Arpad Szendy was one of the last pupils of Liszt. Szendy in turn taught Ilona Kabos who became an important and formidable teacher in London. Nigel recalled, "She tore me to shreds and I felt elevated. She was my mentor for two years." She rarely gave compliments. Nigel reports that Ilona talked about Liszt as if she knew him. "She was steeped in Liszt in a way I never encountered in anyone else. We made a synthesis of music together. When I played the Liszt Sonata for the first time, having keenly listened right through the 29 minutes from her capacious armchair, she arose slowly with a long sigh and grave face, turning back the score with large sweeps of her arm. After several pages and what seemed a very long time she pointed to a precise note and stated triumphantly, 'That note was good!' She was not unkind, but blunt, in a way people with fragile egos couldn't handle. She would state 'That doesn't transport me.' But then when the 'why' came, it opened up new vistas. Ilona asked me to prepare the younger students who came to her for their weekly lessons. I took the opportunity of going to most of their lessons though this was no condition of hers. It was an unbelievable opportunity. She could use a very simple phrase or word that got to the heart of things in the most uncanny way. I always felt liberated by playing for her and Tamas Vasary told me he felt that too. He said she was the ideal audience and he had never had such experiences from other teachers." Clearly Ilona Kabos was Nigel's "holy grail."

While a student, Nigel was known as the best page turner in London. This was his way of getting into the concert hall to hear free performances. Having a page turner you can trust is very important. If the page turner goofs - turning too many pages at once, turning too late, turning too early, or dropping the music, the concert could easily fall apart. Nigel turned pages for Heifetz as well as for Edwin Fischer, Marian Anderson, Kirsten Flagstad, Elizabeth Schwarzkopf, and the composer Francis Poulenc. Poulenc's most humorous performance suggestion to Nigel: "My music is not difficult. Play it in time and drown it with pedal."

Nigel and Eubie

Eubie Blake - a keyboard original.

75

I remember watching Eubie Blake on PBS at the Kennedy Center in the early 1980s. He was almost 100 years old and he could still get around the keyboard. His slim long fingers were agile, even at that advanced age. This was all the more remarkable because Eubie's heyday was at the turn of the last century. I noticed many piano licks in his music that reminded me of Gershwin's piano style. Gershwin of course borrowed and synthesized from many other composers. Eubie complained bitterly that he didn't get enough credit for inventing the ragtime/jazz piano style that was adopted by Gershwin, Zez Confrey and many others in the 1920s. Eubie Blake was a piano original.

Nigel became friends with Eubie's wife, Marion Blake. In her younger days Marion had been the secretary to W.C. Handy. (W.C. Handy is often cited as "The Father of the Blues.") She kindly gave Nigel several piano pieces by Eubie that were unavailable. Nigel scheduled a performance of them at the University of Massachusetts. Unbelievably, on the evening of the performance, Eubie Blake suddenly died, so the concert turned into a Memorial. Carl Selzer, who acted as a kind of secretary to Eubie, later told Nigel he believed Nigel's performance of that music on the evening of Eubie's death was the first time anyone had ever given such a recital devoted to those pieces.

Nigel made a fine recording of *Tricky Fingers* and *Troublesome Ivories* and he generously gave me his copies so I could record them too. We both agreed that these pieces took real work to play well. I had a lot of trouble with *Troublesome Ivories*. Eubie wrote these pieces to show off his virtuosity and unique piano style. They are very effective with an audience and both Nigel and I love playing them in concert.

76

Shura Cherkassky

Shura Cherkassky, another formidable performer.

Nigel knew many of the greats in London, including the legendary Shura Cherkassky. He would often visit Shura at *The White House Hotel* in London. He told me that Shura had a timer and he set it to do four hours of practice every day no matter what. If there were guests at the door or the telephone rang he would stop his timer. He would start the timer only when he returned to the piano. I saw Shura perform when he was in his eighties and there was no question, this guy was rock solid. He launched into a performance of Liszt's *Sonata in B minor* that thrilled us. I remember seeing him on Public

Television for a special live telecast from Carnegie Hall. It was a gala performance with many well-known pianists separately performing one short piece. They mostly didn't play very well. Yes, you read correctly - so I won't mention any names, but I think I know what happened. All these great pianists were back stage at Carnegie Hall, getting caught up with each other, gabbing away, telling jokes and having a good time. All of a sudden it's time to start the concert and no one is really concentrating properly. Playing one little piece at a benefit or a special event of some type can be more difficult and nerve wracking then playing a full length concert - especially if you don't prepare for it mentally. You must leave the scenes of chaos behind you and hone your concentration like a laser, whether for a full length concert, or a five minute appearance. In the case of this Carnegie Hall telecast, everyone is so nervous and flustered. All the pianists walked out on stage, cold, to play one short work. With the cameras rolling everyone tried too hard. "Trying" to play is already wrong. It becomes forced, unnatural and self-conscious. Finally, Shura walked on stage to play the formidable *Kaleidoscope* by his teacher, Josef Hoffman. He played it to perfection. He knocks the ball out of the park with a stunning performance. The audience reacts with pandemonium as if Carnegie Hall had been hit by a thunderbolt. The difference between the previous mediocre performances and Shura's glowing and inspired performance was shocking. An audience may not be able to explain exactly why a performance is great, but they can always tell.

Chapter Five

Filming for PBS

I filmed "Rhapsody in Blue" for my first PBS television show.

In 1994, I was invited to play at the Jewish Community Center, just outside of Springfield, Massachusetts. My program included the Russian composer Modeste Mussorgsky's *Pictures at an Exhibition*. I didn't know that Springfield has a sizeable population of Russian émigrés - but I found out that night. The Russians whooped and hollered after my performance, executed on a beat up old Steinway. Also in attendance was Public Television producer Beth Curley, who decided, after my successful concert, to film me for PBS. I was thrilled. What performer doesn't dream of his own TV show? Unfortunately, a couple months later Newt Gingrich took over Congress with his *Contract on America*. Pardon me, *Contract for America*. Their first act was an attempt to kill PBS. Gingrich and his allies managed to shut down the federal government as well as make PBS scramble for money to keep running. That's it, I thought. My television career is over before it started. A few years later Gingrich resigned because of ethical violations and PBS emerged stronger than ever. I didn't hear from anyone at PBS for two years. To Beth Curley's credit she didn't give up, and finally called me in 1996. She said the problems created by the attempt to destroy PBS had put my project on hold - but now, she finally obtained the funds to go through with the TV show. Hurray!

My old alma mater, the Hartt School, agreed to let us use their facilities for free to make the film. We did this on a shoe-string budget. A couple cameras were borrowed from Aetna Insurance Company (around the corner from where I live) because they actually had better production equipment.

We had two days booked to film. I heard that when you do film work, most of your time is spent waiting. That's usually because of the lighting. It can take as much as two hours to get the lighting right for one camera set-up. The people at PBS liked me, and even invited me back to film more TV shows, because of my patience with the process. I was always ready to perform, and do it over and over without getting tired. Michael Caine, in his book *Acting in Film*, says there is always one problem or another with lighting, camera, or sound. Your job is to make sure you are ready to go as soon as the director and the tech people are ready. The most important part of this work is to be so organized that the director and film crew are not kept waiting.

On the first day of shooting for my first television show we had a snow storm. We arrived at the concert hall with a foot of snow on the ground. This was winter in New England. Luckily, it didn't deter the film crew, but it was so cold outside that the blowers providing heat in the auditorium were working overtime and started to rattle. We had to turn off the heat. I had a portable heater in the green room to keep my hands warm. (I don't know how I dug up a portable heater.) Even with the hot TV lights it must have been 40 degrees in the auditorium and everyone, including the camera men, had on winter coats, winter caps and snow boots. I would run from the green room to the stage when everything was ready, trying to not let my hands get cold. If you carefully watch my performance of *Rhapsody in Blue*, you can see my breath!

I'm a big fan of the RKO films of Fred Astaire. They are marvels. I've been told that many of those spectacular numbers were shot at one in the morning. I can't tell you how many times we have also filmed through midnight just to get a good performance. Set-ups simply take forever but I actually enjoy it. If I'm on a film shoot late at night, I often think of Fred and Ginger making movie magic at one in the morning. When I arrive home at three in the morning I think of Bette Davis who said, "No one knows the sweetness of my joy to arrive home from a hard day of good work."

Phillip Truckenbrod

I finally had my first television show broadcast on PBS in May of 1996. Now I needed a manager - but how to go about it? I sent a copy of the TV show to Edward Jablonski, the much esteemed George Gershwin biographer. He wrote back to me on his old Underwood typewriter (which I thought was quaint) telling me how much he loved the show. Then he wrote, when it came to managers, his colleagues in the music business all agreed, *"When you've got 'em you don't want 'em, when you want 'em you can't get 'em."* His quote, from the lengthy title of that obscure Gershwin song, was not exactly what I wanted to hear. My teacher Luiz also had bad luck with managers. I remained undeterred. I asked Larry Allen Smith, the Dean of the Hartt School, for some advice. He told me he'd put in a word with *Phillip Truckenbrod Concert Artists*, a much respected management agency with an impressive roster of artists.

Phillip Truckenbrod came to a concert of mine and signed me up right away. He has been my manager ever since - the only manager I've ever had. He is the exact opposite of what we usually think of as a manager. He is quiet and low key, with a Midwestern politeness. (He's originally from Iowa.) He wrote up a contract that was generous to me beyond anything I have ever seen in the business. He arranged hundreds of successful concerts for me and helped my career reach a new level, putting the prestige of his agency and its finances behind my career. If there is a constant thread running through this book, it is how much the people we surround ourselves with contribute to our success. Phillip is at the top of that list. He also runs a small recording company. *Towerhill Recordings* was started in the 1960s by Michael Nemo. Tom Richner, a fine pianist, recorded many albums for this company. Phillip revived the company in the mid 1990s and I have recorded 19 CDs under the Towerhill label. As I write these words, Phillip is celebrating the 45th anniversary of *Phillip Truckenbrod Concert Artists*. What a milestone! It just shows that sometimes the good guys do finish first.

Singapore

I got some great news from PBS in 1997 when I heard that China wanted to broadcast my Gershwin television show. The parts of the show where I talk about Gershwin's music were dubbed into Mandarin Chinese and the program was broadcast throughout Asia. The worldwide celebration of the 100th anniversary of Gershwin's birth was coming up in 1998 and I was anxious to participate. The airing of my television show in Asia couldn't have been timed better. It resulted in an engagement with the Singapore Symphony where I was invited to perform *Rhapsody in Blue* as part of the Gershwin Centennial. I was also invited to give some lecture recitals on Gershwin. My friend and former Hartt School classmate Ellen Tryba Chen was teaching in Singapore at the time. She called to tell me that she wanted to personally give me a tour of Singapore. This gleaming city, so safe and friendly, was a delight to explore. It was such a pleasure to make music for people who were so enthusiastic about my concerts. It was also good to reconnect with Ellen. She is such a devoted piano teacher, and every time we get together she has suggestions about new music to teach my students.

Besides all the concerts, Ellen arranged for me to give master classes in Singapore.

Working with the Singapore symphony was a great experience. However, the strict classically trained Asian musicians had some trouble at first feeling the jazz idiom in *Rhapsody in Blue*. In the rehearsals they were slightly stiff. The iconic clarinet opening was written by Gershwin specifically for Ross Gorman, whom Gershwin knew well. Back in the Twenties no one believed that a clarinet could actually do a glissando like that, but Ross could. The original audience in New York was shocked by that wild and riveting opening. When you listen to the original 1924 recording of *Rhapsody in Blue* that Gershwin made for RCA, the opening clarinet solo by Ross Gorman is still shocking. It is deep, rich, clear, loud, and most miraculous of all there is no break in the glissando. It's just one big, perfect slide. Almost no clarinetist can do it that well and the poor clarinetist from the Singapore Symphony, not used to this distinctive American idiom, had to struggle with it.

Filming a Second Television Show for PBS

With the success of my first television show in Asia, as well as America, PBS invited me to film another program. This would be an all-American concert with everything from Gottschalk and Joplin to Billy Joel and John Phillip Sousa. The concert would be filmed live with a studio audience. The set-up was unique - a theater in the round where I would be surrounded by my audience. The nine-foot concert grand was dramatically placed in the middle of the room. The piano was beautifully lit and the inside strings glistened. There were six cameras placed strategically throughout the studio. With the reaction of the live audience right next to me, it made for an inspiring set-up. This was going to be fun.

Backstage exhilaration with nephew Josh Bisaccia and Dianne Hunt Mason, moments after completing a second PBS television show.

Stills from Paul's DVD compilation, Bisaccia on Television.
Clockwise from left: (1) Paul at the Rachmaninoff Room,
Steinway Hall, New York City. (2) A Standing Ovation for Paul's
Second PBS Show. (3) Paul at Nelson Hall in Cheshire CT. (4)
Paul plays Chopin on a Rosewood Steinway from 1896. (5) With
David Giardina. (6) A view from the rafters.

The producers made one small error. Before the taping, an elegant supper was prepared for all the invited guests. In order to keep everyone happy and relaxed, wine was also served. That was a mistake. The audience became too relaxed. The program included one of my favorite Scott Joplin Rags - *Solace*. It reminds me of faded sepia-toned post cards from the turn of the century. It's a masterpiece and a real ragtime lullaby - slow and sweet. Unfortunately, there was a lady in direct view of the most important camera. She had on goggle glasses, which made her stand out even more, and this lullaby made her sleepy. She yawned every fifteen seconds and at the end of the piece simply nodded off. Needless to say, the visuals of an audience member falling asleep while I played live on television were not what we were looking for. When I saw the playback of *Solace,* I realized the number was ruined. It was not possible to edit her out, so the film of this particular number has never seen the light of day. Luckily for the rest of the concert we were able to film around her.

We made a clever commercial for this television concert. The producers managed to find a poster-board with the PBS network logo and placed it prominently on the music rack. I sat at the keyboard and addressed the camera as I pointed to the logo. "I know you all think PBS means *Public Broadcasting Service,* but what it really means is *Paul Bisaccia Special. . .* (beat) it really does!"

Filming Chopin on an Old Steinway

For my Chopin television program we filmed in a unique location. The historic First Congregational Church of West Springfield had gorgeous stained glass windows and a Steinway *Model C* that dated back to 1896. I fell in love with this instrument and I loved the idea of filming Chopin on a piano from the nineteenth century. This particular model had been discontinued by Steinway and it was in exceptionally fine condition. It was made of Rosewood and it was striking in its gleaming, red

87

hued finish. The piano still had the original ivory keys, and best of all, looked exceptional on film.

Besides being a talented crooner, David Giardina directed and produced my Chopin television program.

Before I even thought of filming in this church, I gave a benefit concert to help in the restoration of this fine instrument. This good deed resulted in positive karma for the project. We used the proceeds from the concert to install all new bass strings. The television lights made the new copper strings sparkle, as the cameras filmed the inside of the piano. Before each take I would grab a bottle of Old English Scratch Polish and rub the rosewood finish until it glistened. If you look at some of the film on YouTube you will see what I mean. Luckily, I didn't spill any polish on my concert clothes. For those of you who think how glamorous it is making films, all I can say is - don't forget to bring your furniture polish and a good dust cloth.

Finding the True Sound of the Piano

Rubinstein talks about his search for the true sound of Chopin. He said he was helped by a close friend to find "the true Chopin - the real Polish Chopin." What Rubinstein tells us is important. There is a sound unique to each composer and we must strive for this sound. Sometimes, this sound is found in the metaphysical examination of pressing the key. Rubinstein talks of finding that secret of stroking the key for himself - not too hard, not too soft, but just right, and he says, "I couldn't teach it for all the money in the world." I once gave a lecture at Colby College in Maine titled, "How to Press Down a Piano Key." I gave examples at the keyboard, and used video clips of Arrau, Horowitz, Rubinstein and even Chico Marx to illustrate my points. Why Chico Marx? Just watch some of the clips of Chico playing the piano in those old Marx Brothers movies. The first thing you notice is his total relaxation. Serious pianists could learn something from his ease of execution.

Finding the correct sound from the beginning is crucial. Sometimes I ask a student to play just the first beat of a composition. If you find the most natural way of playing the first notes of a piece, then it's possible to solve the problem of an entire piece. On the other hand, if you can't play the first measure properly, there is no point in continuing. Deepak Chopra, in his book *"The Way of the Wizard"* quotes the Wizard Merlin: "The whole banquet is in the first spoonful." The entire meal is in the first taste. When I am a judge in piano competitions I really don't need to hear more than a few notes to immediately tell a good deal about a performer.

Tim Saternow

I played a concert at the Connecticut Historical Society in 1987. After the concert there was a party at my home and a young set and lighting designer from Yale showed up. His name was Tim Saternow. From the first moment I met him, I knew I wanted him in my circle. It was clear that he was creative, dynamic and headed for success. He worked on Broadway, won an Emmy nomination for a Hallmark Hall of Fame movie, taught around the country, and is currently represented in New York for his watercolor paintings.

At Yale, Tim studied with the set designer Ming Cho Lee. Ming was famous for his work at the Metropolitan Opera and New York Shakespeare Festival. Tim and I had much in common as we discussed our theories about art and our luck to be apprenticed to great teachers - Tim to Ming and me to Luiz.

Tim Saternow taught set and lighting design at both Carnegie Mellon and the University of Connecticut. We often talk about how to help our students. Tim, like so many of the teachers I have studied with, is committed to helping his students learn. One thing he insisted upon with his students: they read the *New York Times Sunday Art Section* from cover to cover. What a superb idea. He would then give a quiz on it every Monday. Many students would complain to Tim about this requirement, only to thank him later.

Tim moved to Seattle in the early nineties when regional theater there was exploding. He created a set design for Tennessee Williams's *A Streetcar Named Desire* that was bold and shocking. There was a perspective to it that was slightly off, just as the world of the play is disjointed and slightly off. I loved visiting Tim in Seattle because the energy there in the nineties was young and exciting. Coffee bars were filled with people discussing books, movies and music. Everyone walked and biked everywhere. Hiking through Mount Rainier was something we did almost every time I came to visit. Looking at the Olympic Mountain Range every day and seeing Mount Rainier in the distance like a big Baked Alaska in the sky inspired me. I spent a summer in Seattle practicing 10 hours a day and all of a sudden my piano playing clicked. I felt like I finally knew what I was doing. I hit my 10,000 hours of practice in Seattle.

A Hot *Appassionata*

I gave my first performance of Beethoven's *Appassionata Sonata* at the Broadway Performance Hall in Seattle. Tim generously volunteered to light the stage for me. His idea was to make the stage all black, except for a brilliant burst of light on me and the piano. I told Tim to go for it. The stage looked riveting and dramatic under his magic lighting - just what I wanted for the *Appassionata*. After my performance under the searing lights I walked off stage dripping wet. The heat from the lights was so intense that I roasted. Tim's reaction made me laugh. "Oh Paul, did I cook you?" Later I made a recording of the *Appassionata*. The author Ann Rice's publisher gave me permission to use her "outside the box" description of this great Sonata for my CD liner notes. This quote is from her book *The Vampire Armand*: "How can human hands make this enchantment, how can they pound out of these ivory keys this deluge, this thrashing, thundering beauty?"

U.S. vs. Hamburg Steinways

In 1996 I recorded two new CDs. The first CD was *Blue Danube: Waltzes by Strauss, Liszt and Chopin*. The second CD was *Ragtime Lullabies*. I recorded both CDs on a Hamburg Steinway at Smith College in Northampton, Massachusetts. This piano was heaven to play. Steinway has factories both in New York and Hamburg, Germany. You can tell just by looking if a piano was made in the Long Island factory or the Hamburg factory. It's the shape of the arms, the part of the case at either end of the keyboard. On a New York Steinway, the curve of the arm ends in a sharp corner. It's called a Sheraton arm, named for Thomas Sheraton, the 18th century furniture designer. On a Hamburg Steinway, the edge is rounded. A hundred years ago New York Steinways had rounded arms too. You can see the rounded arm of a Steinway from 1896 on my Chopin television program. The Sheraton arm (with the sharp corner) was used in the U.S. Steinways starting around 1910. The Hamburg Steinways to this day, use the old-fashioned rounded arms.

There are pianists who prefer a Hamburg Steinway. They say the workmanship is better. On the particular Hamburg Steinway at Smith College I found this to be the case. The dynamic range was wider; the sound was clear, clean and focused. The piano was also more sensitive to my touch. As my finger pushed the key to the bottom, the touch felt solid, even, and direct. There is something about fine German engineering that my hands could feel in this piano. My piano technician said the action in this piano was tight and solid.

When I listen to certain recordings that Rubinstein made for RCA in the 1960s I can tell when he was playing on a Hamburg Steinway. There were many recordings he made at the RCA Italiana studios outside of Rome. The tone (in his Chopin

Waltzes recording for example) made by this particular Hamburg Steinway, has a roundness and more varieties of color. Rubinstein said he loved making recordings at that particular studio. I can hear it immediately in his sound.

Chapter Six

My Champagne Year - Television, Recordings and Provincetown

With Tim Saternow, in front of his diptych, "39 Mott Street."

I call 1996 my "Champagne Year." I managed to film my first Gershwin television show for PBS and record two new CDs (both on that previously mentioned Hamburg Steinway) all in eight months. Sometimes creativity explodes in a burst of activity. That was 1996 for me.

1996 was also my first year living in Provincetown, Massachusetts. Tim Saternow was planning a move up north to start teaching at the University of Connecticut. We decided to rent a cottage in Provincetown for the summer. Tim would use it as a base of operations to search for a house in Connecticut and pursue his watercolors. I would have an inspiring get-away to practice for my CD projects. This was my favorite summer in Provincetown. There was a current of creativity throughout the town which Tim and I both plugged into. Every day Tim would paint, and I would practice the music I was about to record at Smith College. There is something about creating art with friends that inspires and builds on itself. We both made quick progress that summer. Creating art here was a joyful experience. I always advise artists to surround themselves with creative people. Do it and watch new worlds open for you.

An artist's work space is of primary importance. Make sure you have a work space of both beauty and utility. Provincetown is one of the most beautiful places on earth. It has been an artist's colony for over a hundred years and artists flock here to capture the unique light. The harbor is one of the most perfect, natural harbors in the world. On many evenings I would practice as the fog rolled in. There was a street light near the cottage we rented and I can still picture, in my mind, the individual flecks of water vapor blowing past the illumination from the light as I played Chopin. There was magic in the air and it inspired me.

Tim designed CD covers for both of my releases that year. Having an Emmy nominated designer create your covers was an honor. Later, Tim painted a watercolor that captured the moon coming up over Cape Cod Bay on Beach Point. I used that painting for my *Clair de Lune* CD and I think it's my favorite cover. The cover is so stunning that when people ask me to sign CDs for them I feel guilty marking it up with my signature. My father bought another painting by Tim of Beach Point at low tide which still hangs in my parents' home. Tim now has a studio in New York City and I love visiting his studio to check out his works in progress. For a musician, being connected to the other arts is important. We often talk about the interconnectedness of the arts. To be an artist you need to have an interest in all of life - books, movies, food, art, religion, and politics. Put it all under a microscope and use it to inspire you.

Writers as Inspiration

With Oscar and Emmy nominated designer Leslie Rollins, Emmy nominated designer Tim Saternow and vocalist Ken Browne, attending New York gallery opening of new paintings by Tim Saternow.

Rubinstein said it was always writers and books that attracted him. When he was living in Paris, in the 1920s, he spent his time in the cafés with tables of writers. Tony Randall, in his book on Hollywood, says the same thing. If you wanted to be where the conversation was the most interesting at the MGM studio commissary you sat at the writers' table. Certainly the Liszt school also attracted creative writers. Franz Liszt himself wrote books and monographs. Robert Schumann ran a magazine and was constantly writing for it. Liszt found inspiration for his major piano works from the works of authors. *Mephisto Waltz* (Goethe's Faust), *Vallée d'Obermann* (Etienne de Senacourt), *Dante Sonata* (Dante), *Consolations* (Sainte-Beuve), *Sonata in B minor* (Goethe's Faust). The list is large.

Michael Cunningham, who won the Pulitzer Prize for the book *The Hours* actually wrote his celebrated book down the street from me here in Provincetown. During Christmas week, Tim and I were relaxing in Provincetown. After dinner in town one night, we returned to my condo and Tim put some sheet music on the piano rack as a surprise. It was Phillip Glass's score to *The Hours*. I hadn't seen the movie yet which starred Meryl Streep, Julianne Moore and Nicole Kidman, but Tim had, and he raved about both the movie and the book. Tim lit some candles and asked me to play the score. Thirty miles out in the middle of the Atlantic Ocean, with the twinkling of the Christmas tree lights, on a deserted Beach Point, this haunting score inspired me. I read the score at sight, and with such pleasure, that I decided immediately to record some of the music on my next CD project.

As Michael Cunningham wrote *The Hours*, he constantly played recordings of the music of Phillip Glass for inspiration. Cunningham wanted Glass to do the movie score, but Glass declined, so another composer was hired. A glitch occurred and the original composer left the project. Suddenly, Glass became available. Happily, after this comedy of errors, Phillip Glass was ultimately hired by the movie producers to write the score. The music and the film mesh perfectly. It is rare when this happens.

The movie received nine Academy Award nominations and Glass was nominated for Best Score.

Later that season, pianist and concert producer John Thomas arranged the annual "Celebration of Life" which is a free end-of-season concert for all the locals in Provincetown. I was invited to perform, and then there was a surprise guest. Michael Cunningham got up on stage, and read an excerpt from his new book *Land's End - a walk in Provincetown*. I was pleased to find that Michael is as big a fan of Provincetown as I am. In his book he calls Provincetown, "eccentric, physically remote, and heartbreakingly beautiful."

Just to prove yet again that "six degrees of separation" has become two degrees of separation in the arts: My friend Leslie Rollins won an Academy Award nomination for his set decoration in a movie with Matt Damon called *The Good Shepherd*. His success brought him work on the movie *The Manchurian Candidate* featuring Meryl Streep who was so unforgettable in *The Hours*. Leslie told me that Streep would say to the director, "I can play this scene ten different ways. Just tell me which way you want me to do it." That is creativity and true virtuosity. Remember it when we get to the section on making recordings.

Listening to Other Pianists

In Stephen King's book *On Writing* he says, "If you want to be a writer, you must do two things above all others: read a lot and write a lot. There's no two ways around these two things that I'm aware of, no shortcut." I say if you want to be a concert pianist, you must do two things above all others: perform a lot and listen to other pianists a lot. Listening to the recordings of the great pianists of the past is part of the work. For starters, I would recommend hearing the entire recorded repertoire of Rubinstein, Horowitz and Rachmaninoff. These three giants of the piano present a compendium of the best piano playing around. All three have a point of view and a unique sound. Rubinstein's is probably the simplest and straight forward. Spend some time trying to imitate his direct sound and see if your piano playing improves. However, I wouldn't recommend trying to imitate Horowitz too much. His sound is so unique and idiosyncratic that trying to imitate it becomes a distortion of the music. Horowitz can get away with his eccentricities because he is a genius. Most others cannot.

Some musicians do not want to listen to other artists for fear of imitation. I'm not one of them. I love to hear other inter-pretations - it opens up possibilities. If you like a performance, let the good parts of it seep into your subconscious. In books and movies, artists like Stephen King and Meryl Streep freely admit to borrowing as part of their craft. They put it through their personal filter and make it their own. Let borrowing from others become part of your toolbox of possibilities, just like Stephen King and Meryl Streep do in preparing their work.

Prague

Tim Saternow invited me to the Prague Quadrennial in June of 2003, just as the U.S. was gearing up for the ill-fated war in Iraq. The Quadrennial was sponsored by the Czech Government. There were set, costume and lighting designers (both students and teachers) from all over the world - the Middle East, Asia, Latin America, Asia, Europe and Australia. The theater designs were displayed in a massive exhibition hall in Prague.

As we visited Prague, the impending war weighed heavily on our minds. As we met with and experienced the work of so many talented artists and students from all over the world, I thought no one who had the chance to experience other cultures and ways of thinking would make the tragic mistake of war in Iraq. There is a long history of theater works about war going back to ancient Greece. Ironically, some of the set designs for these works were displayed in Prague on our visit which made us ponder the issue even further. Perhaps our leaders need to have a more broad based knowledge of the humanities. Wars are always a tragedy and almost always a mistake.

Prague is known as the Paris of the East. It wasn't destroyed during World War II and there is much that is very old. There was a church down the street from our hotel that dated back to 800 AD. There is a Jewish section of the city with a cemetery and synagogues dating back to the 13th century. With Tim's vast knowledge of periods of art, he was the ultimate tour guide.

While in Prague we saw *Don Giovanni* performed to perfection in the Estates Theater. This was the actual theater where it was first staged, conducted by Mozart himself on October 19, 1787. During the Soviet occupation of Prague the theater became a storage facility. When Milos Forman directed the Academy Award winning movie *Amadeus*, he actually staged and filmed sequences of *Don Giovanni* in the long abandoned Estates Theater. He had art directors recreate and restore the theater to its former glory. This being the movies, all the sumptuous gold inlays and designs are fake. Tim having worked on movies, explained to me that what we saw was made of plastic and not real golden sculptures. You are dazzled by the beauty of this gem of a hall. It is tiny and you realize Mozart operas were created for these intimate venues. It is a lesson in how to approach Mozart piano sonatas as well. You must convey great power (such as in Mozart's *A minor Piano Sonata*) but on this smaller Mozartean scale. Mozart loved Prague and said the days he spent there were among the happiest in his life. The city has always had a reputation as being incredibly musical, even before Mozart's day. That has been my experience as well.

*Martin Kasik - one of my favorite
performers.*

The city really does overflow with musicality. I love
musicians from Prague because just as in Mozart's day, they are
true musicians who have a special gift for phrasing and beauty
of sound. I heard Rudolf Firkusny perform live and his sound at
the piano was sensuous and beautiful, like none I'd ever heard.
Elegant and patrician are the words that come to mind. One of
my absolute favorite pianists from Prague performing today is
Martin Kasik. Martin lives in Prague, but has a career all over
the world. He won the Prague Spring International Competition

in 1998. He then came to the U.S. and won the Young Concert Artists Competition in New York in 1999. I will be performing some four-hand piano music with him in the 2013 season and I can't wait. He really is the star of the young generation of Czech pianists, but he is more than that. His musicality is such that my friend, the pianist Nigel Coxe, raved. He said the concert of Martin's, that we both attended, was the best he heard all year.

Corbin Beisner

As musicians we must always be planning ahead. Some counterintuitive planning is part of Corbin's story. Corbin comes from Las Vegas where his father was the pianist with the Maynard Ferguson Orchestra. During his senior year at Hartt, Corbin gave several recitals. One of the concerts contained most of the Liszt *Transcendental Etudes* - a huge feat. The difficulty in performing a concert of that magnitude is the sheer amount of notes and the wall of sound the piano produces. It is possible for the audience to get fatigued with all that sound. Corbin managed to overcome this danger because of his tremendous technique and the organic way he allowed the music to evolve. The sound was structured and focused. When Liszt called his Etudes "Transcendental" he made clear that the staggering technique required to play these pieces is a means to a spiritual end. You need to make these pieces more than pieces to show off - there is a deep spiritual core to them. Corbin keeps winning prizes every time he enters competitions and with good reason. He has a technical accuracy that is astonishing, combined with an easy relaxed way at the keyboard.

Corbin Beisner - one of the best of the new generation of pianists.

After his senior recital he was invited, all expenses paid, to do graduate studies at the University of Arkansas - a wonderful honor. Normally I never interfere with decisions such as this, but after hearing Corbin play as he does, both Luiz and I told him he shouldn't go to Arkansas. My reasoning was simple. Corbin is the real deal and when you do graduate degrees you spend too much time in libraries, writing papers, doing research, teaching or taking classes. What musicians really need is time to themselves, to think and practice. That 10,000 hours that Malcolm Gladwell talks about in *Outliers* is crucial. Also, Corbin studied with Luiz with such spectacular results. Staying on this path, and staying in an area so important for music (the Boston - New York corridor) really made sense. If you have an opportunity to hear Corbin in concert, run - don't walk to hear him.

Jason Meyer

I've performed in concert with Jason Meyer for almost forty years. Our latest CD together has just been released.

Martha Argerich said, "Jason Meyer is a marvelous composer and a great violinist." I agree. It is a feast to make music with him.

Jason and I grew up in East Hartford together. One of the perks of getting older is the way people you have known and worked with for years become family. Jason and I have been playing concerts together since the mid 1970s. He is now a concert violinist and composer living in Paris. If you happen to visit Paris and turn on your television set, you may actually hear Jason's music on French television. We just finished recording a new CD together of music by Franck and Gershwin. We also recorded Jason's fiery new composition *Odessa*. This piece is a homage to his grandparents who were Russian immigrants.

For this recording session, Jason flew in from Paris and we had an evening rehearsal. The next day Jason went before the microphones with his exquisite *Zamberti* violin and we made our recording. With certain musicians little rehearsal is needed, and it is a wonderful way to capture an inspired performance. For the spring of 2013 we plan to release our latest CD and perform concerts in the States and in Paris.

I love the sound of Jason's violin. I recently told him of an NPR broadcast comparing Stradivarius violins to modern instruments. The premise was that new violins are approaching the quality of Strads. I disagree with that premise. A new study showed that college violin teachers could not tell the difference between the Strads and certain new violins when they listened to them in blind tests. At the end of the broadcast the reporter played recordings of two different violins. I was driving and cranked up the volume in my car to listen carefully. In three seconds I knew the first violin they played was a Stradivarius. I could hear immediately what I like to call the "honey" in the sound.

Why didn't the violin teachers hear the difference? The answer is simple. Not all violin teachers (or piano teachers for that matter) have made a careful analysis of the sound of the instrument. Just like a person can be taught to look for the various components in a complex bottle of wine, (hints of vanilla, chocolate and berries for instance) we can be taught to identify the components of a complex sound whether in a Stradivarius or a Steinway. I told this story to Jason and we Googled the radio broadcast. Of course Jason could also tell which violin was the Strad immediately. Maybe the study should have been done with active concert violinists and not violin teachers.

This brings me to another story about careful listening: a college professor once said to me, "Anyone, even my ten year old daughter, can play a single note on the piano just as well as Rubinstein. It is how the notes are connected that is the secret of great piano playing." I think the assertion by this college professor is mistaken. While it is true that Rubinstein has a great legato (the smoothness of the connection between notes) the innate sound of each individual note he creates is unique. If we looked at the sound waves generated on the computer from one single note by Rubinstein, and one note generated by a random person off the street, I guarantee you the visuals of the Rubinstein sound would be fatter and richer. There is a way of depressing a key which generates a warmer, thicker, more focused sound. It is difficult and takes tremendous knowledge and concentration. Very few people can do it well. If you listen to my teacher Luiz's newest CD (from the concert reviewed by Alan Walker in this book) check out his hair-raising performance on that disc of Liszt's *Funérailles*. The very first note (a low D-flat) has a deepness and penetration of sound unique to Luiz's way of playing. The quality of the tone Luiz creates is not just found in the connection between the notes,

107

but exists inside the notes themselves. This quality makes Luiz's recording of *Funérailles* one of the best available anywhere.

David Giardina

I've performed in concert with David Giardina all over the U.S.

I met David while hiking in Vermont. My two favorite places on earth are Cape Cod and the rolling hills of Vermont. Several people told me that David was a guy I should meet. We arranged to have dinner together to talk about music and it turned out we had much in common. He has a crooner's voice and is crazy about the music of the '20s and '30s. He's also a writer, filmmaker and actor living in New York. He invited me to accompany him for a benefit at the United Nations. My manager heard the musical results and packaged us on his concert roster as *Tin Pan Alley - Alive!* David had won the Best Director Award at the New York International Independent Film Festival in Los Angeles and Audience Choice Award for Best Feature at the same festival in New York for his direction of the thriller, *Taffy was Born*. It was a natural progression to talk about making some films of my performances.

David arranged to film me playing a good chunk of my repertoire at Steinway Hall in New York, and venues around New England. Few concert pianists are privileged to have their work captured on film for posterity. It was a great moment for me to have the DVD of our films presented to the public. Working with David on this project impressed me. He does not give up until he gets what he wants. We were filming until one in the morning on many nights - trying to get just the right camera angles. Indeed we had our camera man, Chris Pirelli, climbing a scaffold and holding a camera steady for so long that his hand almost fell off in the attempt to get a unique angle from high above the stage. You can see one of those camera angles as the header for my concert web site.

David loves *The Great American Songbook*. It's ironic that he ended up living in the neighborhood known as *Tin Pan Alley* in New York City where all this great music was created. The name *Tin Pan Alley* originally referred to a specific place: West 28th Street between Fifth and Sixth Avenue, and a plaque on the sidewalk on 28th Street between Broadway and Sixth, commemorates it. Hundreds of pianists flocked to Tin Pan Alley and they all had pianos in their offices. Their goal was to compose a song hit. The racket created by hundreds of pianists banging away at their pianos made a commotion. It sounded as if hoards of people were banging on pots and pans. *The New York Herald* dubbed this area of New York *Tin Pan Alley* and the name stuck. As a teenager, Gershwin was a song *plugger* for the music publishing house *Remicks*. He had a reputation as a genius from the beginning. His tricky virtuoso piano style was already developed by the time he was 16 and he could play anything. As a song *plugger*, he was paid fifteen dollars per week. His job was to play the latest tunes to customers, trying to get them to purchase the sheet music. One of those regular customers was the young Fred Astaire, who would visit George in his piano cubicle, looking for new music to incorporate into his act with his sister Adele. When I visit Dave in New York I always remember that the Gershwins, Irving Berlin, Eubie Blake, and all those other legendary composers, hung out in *Tin Pan Alley*. They walked the very streets where I walk so often myself.

Making Recordings

Rubinstein always said you should become your own best teacher - especially when you make recordings. When it was time to listen to the play-backs of his recordings, Rubinstein would light his cigar and tell Max Wilcox, his producer, "And now I take my piano lesson." He considered making recordings as the best way to learn and improve. I've always felt that making recordings or films of your work is better than earning a doctorate in piano, and it's better for your bank account too. The constant work before a microphone forces you to listen carefully and judge every facet of your own work. We can always play better. My first rule for making recordings is preparation. Time is money in a recording studio and anything you can do to make your job and the recording engineer's job easier and less time consuming is important.

Here's my to-do list and reminders to myself when I record:

1. Have a list of the works to record and their timings, with a copy for the recording engineer, in the order you want to record them.

2. Bring your own headphones. You should be used to them and know what the sound should be. Then you don't have to make comparisons with different headphones when you listen to playbacks.

3. Bring comfortable clothes - I always pack a sweater. Sometimes these concert halls get chilly.

4. Wait at least four seconds after a take. Try not to move or make any sound after you are done. That sound can still reverberate in the hall and you want to hear just the sound of the room at the end of a piece. Rubinstein tells the story of recording *Navarra* by Albeniz, one of his favorite encores. Against his better judgment he invited some friends to the recording studio. As Rubinstein tells it, he gave the best performance of his life and at the rousing finale his friends cheer and scream bravo. The perfect take is ruined and he didn't have the heart to attempt another performance that day.

5. The music must be thoroughly prepared. Like Meryl Streep before the cameras, you must have several versions ready to go before the microphones. Be prepared to change your interpretation if it doesn't sound right. You must be able to play in a way that the microphones approve. By that I mean don't over-accent or over-play. What sounds exciting in a concert hall may sound over-played on a recording. In concert, Rubinstein

let the excitement of the moment allow him to play in a different way than in his recordings. In recordings, especially his later ones, his playing became simpler and even more direct and beautiful - all exaggeration was eliminated. I would go so far as to say his recordings in old age are some of the most beautiful piano playing ever captured for posterity. Simplicity was his credo.

6. The mikes pick up everything, including your breathing or your nail accidentally clicking against a key. My piano tuner sitting close to the piano during a take crossed his leg. I was playing some intimate Debussy and the woosh of the fabric on his pants was picked up by the mikes. I had to redo the piece. When the old analog recordings are digitized and reissued, if you listen to a playback on very sensitive head phones, you can hear this type of problem clearly. I can hear Rubinstein's sinus problem or Arrau's nail clicking. You don't hear this at all on the old vinyl recordings but you can hear it on the digitally remastered recordings. Hopefully all clicks and buzzes in the piano are eliminated before the recording session begins.

7. It is amazing how different touches or ways to depress a piano key show up defects in the piano itself. I often joke with my piano tuner that I can find a problem with a piano that no one else can, because I have so many different ways of striking a key. Sometimes a certain way of striking a key will illicit an extraneous sound. My piano technician will work on the piano the day before the recording session so we do not waste time on the day of the session. Sounds from the piano bench or the pedals are always a headache. I always tell my piano tuner to check out the bench and pedals before I get there. I always try to have a rug underneath the bench, and I wear sneakers instead of shoes to soften the sound of my foot on the pedal.

8. Sometimes the soft pedal doesn't line up properly. If that's the case you can get the sound of one hammer hitting two different notes. Remind the piano tuner to check for that. Another name for the soft pedal is the *una corda* pedal. (Una corda means one string.) This una corda pedal is the furthest to the left. When it is depressed the keyboard actually shifts over about a quarter of an inch. As the keyboard shifts over, the hammers shift over. The hammers are now aligned to strike less of the strings. The sound is a lovely special effect, somewhat like the plink of a harp. If the pedal is adjusted just right, there is a special ping on every note. I need to hear the ping, so I insist on this pedal being adjusted properly.

9. Get the best recording engineer you can find. My recording engineer, James LeGrand, was an assistant on one of my very first recordings. In fact, he was just a teenager when we started working together. He went to a recording technology school and came back as a sound expert. I have been working with him now for almost two decades. He doesn't run out of energy, and is willing to work with me from early in the morning until late at night to get everything right. When you find someone who is willing to put in hours like that, you keep him. I always laughed when Rubinstein said he never ran out of energy. He would keep going until five in the morning. Everyone else would be limping across the finish line and Rubinstein was always, as he put it, "fresh as a daisy" when he made recordings.

10. Get the best piano technician you can find. My piano technician and I go back even further than my recording engineer. I bought my first Steinway in 1974 - a gorgeous mahogany Model A Steinway made in 1900 with scroll work and the original ivory keys. I needed a piano technician. I saw an ad in the Yellow Pages for a guy who lived close by. This was pure

luck. Chris Robinson walked into my house, set eyes on my prized piano and said, "You know, I just love working on these old babies." I knew right away that I had a winning technician who was as passionate about pianos as I was.

Chris was inducted into the Piano Technician's Hall of Fame - and with good reason. We pianists all love those Renner hammers from Germany that are now put in most high end grand pianos. Chris contributed to the design of a long, blank molding that would enable the installer to face the hammer in its most advantageous position, and to fit the string heights of the piano perfectly - two requirements that had not been previously possible with even the replacement hammers from the actual piano manufacturers themselves. Permitting the perfect positioning of the hammer in the piano action resulted in the best tonal response. Now the hammers could be customized to the requirements of each individual instrument. Chris also mastered the fine art of piano rebuilding. He rebuilt my Steinway model A and later a model B made in 1926. He has also done the piano prep work for most of my CDs and my first TV show for PBS.

Acousticraft, the piano restoration company founded by Chris is now in the capable hands of another Chris - Chris Haberbosch. Chris H. just helped me with my newest CD, *Masterworks!* I was so happy with the sound quality in this recording. Chris said it was really a challenge to work on this CD project because we pushed the envelope on getting my 1926 Steinway to play and sound perfectly. We spent almost two full days just tuning the piano, voicing the hammers and making sure the dampers were all correct. It's amazing how much time it takes. Careful listening and a refined sense of sound is required.

114

It is easy to wreck a piano with constant use. When Chris Robinson comes to my home to do some repair work, he looks at me with an arched eyebrow and the first thing he says is, "Now what have you done to my piano?" Rubinstein put it another way: "All these talented men and women - piano technicians who devote their lives to the noble craft of making these pianos play with the utmost perfection - and what do we pianists do to these fine instruments? DESTROY THEM!"

A Harrowing Trip to Brazil

My second concert tour of Brazil was in May of 1998, just after I bought my home on the Cape. I had an itinerary that included major cities throughout Brazil including Rio, Brasilia, Curitiba, and Fortaleza. As we left Kennedy Airport I had a sense of foreboding. About 30 minutes into the flight over the Atlantic Ocean, I looked out my window and saw flames licking the engines. A few seconds later the pilot announced we would be returning to Kennedy Airport. As we circled the airport a crew of fire trucks and ambulances were stationed on the ground below. All I could think was, I had just bought a wonderful home on Cape Cod and would never see it again. Luckily we managed to land safely. For some reason I was chosen to be placed on another flight leaving within minutes. I arrived in Sao Paulo, only to realize that my complicated airline itinerary had been canceled by the computers. I was brought to an office in the airport where a kind airline official was able to reconstitute my itinerary - but I had to rush to get on a flight to Curitiba. I hurried to my flight and only realized, after we took off, that I had left my passport on the desk of the airline official in Sao Paulo. He needed my passport to fix my itinerary, but he neglected to return it. I arrived in Curitiba, with no luggage and no passport. Luckily, my hosts rescued me, and the airport official in Sao Paulo cleared everything up. I gave a concert that day in sneakers - my concert shoes and tux were still in transit from New York.

I flew to Brasilia the next day. The concert hall was close to my hotel so I simply walked there. I was warned by my hostess to be careful. As a blond American I stood out, and if I walked on a side street or took any detours I might not return. The concert went well and at the after-concert party I mentioned how much I was looking forward to Rio. One fellow at the party said ominously, "If I were you, I would be very careful in Rio." I said, "I'm used to cities. I walk all over New York." He said even more ominously "New York is kindergarten compared to Rio." I thought he was exaggerating.

The next day I flew to Rio. It was thrilling to see Sugarloaf and the gleaming city of Rio de Janeiro as we flew towards the airport. After landing, usually I'm met at the airport by a concert representative. In this case no one was there so I grabbed a taxi. I was warned that this could be problematic, but I made it to my hotel without incident. I had three hours before my concert. I was comfortably set up in my hotel room and decided to take a quick stroll on Copacabana Beach before heading to the concert hall. Three minutes on the beach and I was surrounded by five guys who put their arms around me and walked with me, acting like I was their best friend - except one of them had a knife which he positioned against my stomach. They wanted every-thing. Luckily, they couldn't tell that my possessions were worthless. They only looked expensive. I had a Wal-Mart watch worth five dollars and a necklace worth only sentimental value. They took those items and ran off. For some reason I wasn't really shaken up. I just didn't have the time to process it. The concert promoter laughed when I told her what happened - "typical Rio" she said. I gave my concert and luckily played well. It was only later that I became more nervous about walking by myself in Rio. When I returned to the United States I was relieved to be in one piece.

Chapter Seven

Cape Cod

Even though we've had relatives on the Cape since the early 20th century, my first time on the Cape was June of 1969. Entering the Cape changed my life and captured my imagination. We would skin-dive in the bay and pretend we were Jacques Cousteau as hundreds of fish swam past our masks. My brothers and cousins and I would hike in the dunes, swim for hours at the Coast Guard Beach and Race Point. I still never tire of the rolling acres of beach grass, dunes, and expansive bay which I'm actually looking at now as I type these words from my kitchen table.

My parents retired in Eastham close to the Salt Pond Visitors Center. The Audubon Bird Sanctuary was in their back yard. I would bring up a digital piano to practice on my parents' porch. One day I was practicing the Liszt *Valse Oubliée*. (There are a set of four of them and I believe I was the first person to actually record all four. The fourth Waltz of the set was actually discovered in 1955.) At the end of these waltzes are chains of trills up in the high register of the piano. They sound like little bird calls. As I was practicing, I noticed that several birds were joining in and trying to sing with my trills. Soon there were dozens and then hundreds of birds creating a tremendous din. They chirped in a huge cacophony of sound that actually made the earth rumble. My astonished parents came running out onto the porch to see what was happening. By now there were over a thousand birds in the back yard. It was surreal - like something from Alfred Hitchcock's *The Birds*. These pieces must have some type of wonderful organic effect on wild life. Even now at my home in Provincetown as I practice, the birds seem to always show up when I play. Liszt also composed a Legend titled *St Francis Preaching to the Birds*. I shudder to think what might occur if I actually played this music at the bird sanctuary.

I bought my home on Cape Cod in 1998. It is actually on Beach Point - a little sand bar on the Provincetown/Truro border. There must have been some sixth sense at work when I decided to purchase my home. I'm actually a big believer in gut reactions. About one minute into the initial inspection I said, "Let's go to your office right now and sign the papers!" My real estate agent's mouth dropped. My intuition said that purchasing this condo was the right move for me. The day I took possession of my new home on Cape Cod, I placed my key in the lock to open the door. As I turned the lock, I looked towards Truro and saw a rainbow across the horizon. I have taken that rainbow to be a special omen and it hasn't let me down. Provincetown is paradise.

The next step after purchase of my home was to get a piano out there. My home is actually on the top floor of a condo so I had to be imaginative. Many people thought I was crazy to even attempt it, but luckily, I found a guy in town with a crane. He said he'd come with the crane on his lunch hour. I arranged to have a nice, shiny, new baby grand delivered from Hartford to my doorstep in Provincetown, at noon. All the neighbors gathered to watch the sight of a grand piano flying through the air, attached to the crane with cables, and landing, gently, on my deck. My mom and dad came from Eastham to watch the event, but my mom got nervous as the piano floated through the air. She ran to the back bedroom screaming, "I can't watch, I can't watch!" The piano was easily moved in and the legs were attached. The whole operation took about 20 minutes.

I positioned the piano so as to have an excellent view of the bay. On a clear day I can see 30 miles across, all the way to Brewster, Massachusetts. I love practicing with this view. It makes my phrases more expansive and I like to think that the fresh sea air makes my phrases breathe. In the winter most of Beach Point is closed down, so I am often the only person out there. I can bang away at midnight. It's just me and the coyotes howling away against the winter wind. I've done the prep for most of my CDs out there on Beach Point. I've written most of this book here too and I think, just like all the authors and painters who have come here for inspiration, that some of my inspiration has come from the magic of the Outer Cape. Pulitzer Prize winning author and Provincetown resident Michael Cunningham aptly calls my neighborhood one of those "strangely potent places."

John Thomas

John Thomas is another example of a musician who thinks outside the box. He's a lawyer, composer, pianist, actor, writer, activist and has become a legend on the Outer Cape. I think John's many diverse talents make his music more exciting and vital. He produces dozens of concerts a year and has helped make the tiny community of Provincetown a destination for music. John accompanies everyone in town and manages to keep up a hectic schedule of students and performances. The concert that everyone always talks about is the *Celebration of Life* concert that John has produced every year since 1994. It's a free concert that occurs the weekend after Labor Day and the entire town shows up. In this supportive, nurturing atmosphere surrounded by the natural beauty of one of the most beautiful towns in the world, a miracle happens. Musicians filled with inspiration play and sing in a way they never did before. I have heard some of the best performances of the season at this one concert. There is a reason that Provincetown is a special place for artists, musicians, photographers and writers. We like to boast that there are more Pulitzer Prizes awarded to people in the Outer Cape community than anywhere else.

John Thomas - a Provincetown original. (Photo credit: Brad Fowler)

John has a great sense of humor and is a fine improviser at the keyboard. Together John and I have done many concerts for charity on the Cape. We titled these concerts *"Four Hands, Two Guys, One Piano."* John wrote a special four-hand ditty for our appearances together and called it *Dirty Rag.* It has turned into his trademark. The concerts have become so successful that we couldn't resist making a recording of it. We are planning a new CD release for 2013 of four-hand American piano music including seldom played music by Gottschalk and Eubie Blake.

In August of 2010, Provincetown celebrated the 100th anniversary of the Pilgrim Monument. This is the largest all-granite structure in North America and it can be seen from vantage points all over the Outer Cape. Provincetown is proud of the fact that the Pilgrims first landed here several months before they went on to Plymouth Rock. They also signed the *Mayflower Compact* in the harbor here. This was the first governing document of democracy in the Western Hemisphere. Thousands came in 2010 to help celebrate the anniversary of the Pilgrim Monument with music, speeches and fireworks. John's original composition, *I Hear America Singing* (with words by Walt Whitman) was performed by the Outer Cape Chorale Chamber Singers. John also wrote his *Variations on Amazing Grace* just for me, to help mark the occasion. I was so grateful to John for his effective piano arrangement. I've played it in dozens of concerts throughout the country and recorded it on my *Great American Piano Revisited* CD.

A stage with a Steinway Grand was erected at the base of the Pilgrim Monument for the anniversary grand finale and I was invited to play *Rhapsody in Blue* and *The Stars and Stripes Forever*. As I played the last triumphant chord, from the greatest of Sousa Marches, fireworks rocketed over the harbor.

Katherine Foy

Katherine Foy was a concert pianist based in New York City and Cape Cod. I like to describe her by saying, "Picture Katherine Hepburn as a concert pianist and then you will know what

Katherine Foy was like." Kitty (as she was known) was a favorite guest of Arthur Fiedler and the Boston Pops. She was also a Fulbright Scholar. She last played with the Pops under Keith Lockhart around 2003. Kitty had a compound not too far from the Kennedy Compound in Hyannis on the Cape. Her amazing estate consisted of two homes of moderate size, and a great mansion right on the water. (She lived in one of the smaller homes over the summertime and rented the mansion out to a Hollywood director.) There was a beautiful Steinway Grand Piano in each of the two homes (she referred to them as cottages) and a third Steinway in the sumptuous living room of her mansion. This piano was in front of two French doors which opened to the Atlantic Ocean. There was a gigantic fireplace in the living room with an oil painting of a stormy sea above the mantle. Her husband, Louis Foy was a writer for Agence France-Presse. He was the reporter who actually first transmitted the news to Europe of the death of President Kennedy in 1963.

Kitty invited me to give concerts in her home and what a thrill that was. It actually gave me the idea to have my own home with a grand piano looking out over the ocean. In Kitty's home I played all-Chopin concerts and Gershwin concerts too. Luiz was invited to give a memorable series of master classes and concerts in her home. I will never forget one inspiring afternoon watching Luiz rehearse the Franck *Prelude Chorale and Fugue*. The piece built up to a wall of sound - thick and thunderous as Luiz forcefully seized the notes like the claws of a lion would seize its prey. With the last notes still clanging and the smoke clearing from the piano he looked at me directly and said wide-eyed, "Now that's commitment!"

Labor Day on the Cape was always special to the locals because it was the day that hordes of tourists would pack up and go home. The Cape would seemingly revert to a quieter, calmer place in just one day. Many locals breathed a sigh of relief. I mentioned that Kitty would rent out her Cape Cod mansion for the summer to a Hollywood director. Just before Labor Day one of her guests remarked - "Oh Kitty, it will be so lonely for you without us after Labor Day. Whatever will you do when we leave?" Kitty's one word answer á la Hepburn: "FUMIGATE!"

Science and Music

A frequent guest of Kitty's at the concerts on the Cape was a scientist, engineer and inventor friend of mine. His name is Eric Hildebrant and he is a physics researcher at M.I.T. in Cambridge, Massachusetts. He comes from a family of scientists and engineers. Like Luiz, Eric at age ten was already studying calculus. Everyone in the world loves the cameras that are in most cell phones today. Eric and his team developed that technology in the mid to late '80s. His discoveries and ingenuity led to his receiving the *Patent of the Year Award*.

Eric is also an amateur musician. He would get inspired by the music and the beautiful views of the ocean. Later he would tell me, as we walked on the beach, that a new idea for an electrical circuit just came to him and he would have to write it down. Here again is an example of music and science going together. Eric told me that inventing is just as much art as science. He needs the beauty of the ocean to think and clear his mind. This clearing of the mind is the important point for creative people. Important ideas often spring from the unconscious and quiet contemplative spaces can be just the place to access these unconscious inspirations.

When Luiz was foreman of the jury for the Van Cliburn

competition, he told me of a medical student who entered the Cliburn Competition and played the piano better than most of the piano majors. The ability of some people to communicate through music is not something we understand completely. The connections that lay the foundation for great music making are mysterious and varied, but medicine and music seem to be intimately connected. I have taught several students who were medical doctors. Symphonies and conservatories always seem to have doctors on their boards.

In high school my best friend was a typical engineer type who played sax and clarinet - Ed Gacek. We were constantly listening to music together and performed in all the typical venues in our high school. I remember how much we both loved the Copland *Clarinet Concerto* which at that time was a new masterpiece. I remember listening to albums like Bernstein's *West Side Story* and *Judy Garland at Carnegie Hall* with Ed. Even now when I hear these recordings I'm brought back to the hours we spent hanging out in the family rec room listening to these recordings over and over. Ed almost followed me into music, but he ended up double majoring in biological and chemical engineering at the University of Pennsylvania while I double majored in piano performance and education. I really became aware of this connection between music and science during my high school days and it was no coincidence that I almost became a marine biologist.

After getting his degrees in chemical and biological engineering, Ed decided to become a medical doctor. We all know how grueling it is to get accepted into med school. The committees looking for candidates for these schools want people who are well rounded. Ed had an interview at George Washington University and it turned out that the doctor who interviewed him loved music. Ed's knowledge of music helped him in the interview process and he was accepted. He went on to become a wonderful doctor as well as an inspiring teacher himself and currently is chief of medicine in Port Angeles on the Olympic Peninsula in Washington State. I flew up to perform there just last year.

One final anecdote on the subject of science and music: Raya Garbousova often told us this story with relish. Albert Einstein was an amateur violinist who loved to play quartets and trios. Garbousova and Isaac Stern were playing with Einstein who kept getting lost in the music. Finally, an exasperated Stern screams out to the discoverer of the Theory of Relativity, "No, no, Professor, can't you count? ONE, TWO, THREE!"

Kids and Pets

When I'm practicing in Provincetown, a crowd of children and their parents will sometimes congregate on the fence below my deck. I enjoy the applause from my neighbors after I finish the run through of a piece. Now and then parents will bring their young children up to see the piano. I'll open up the lid and let the children peek inside, check out the hammers, golden harp and strings. I love their sense of wonder as they watch me play. I'm sure that was the sense of wonder I had when I was four years old.

I've always enjoyed animals and many animals seem to love the piano too. I had a dog that would lie at my feet as I practiced. I sometimes give lessons to children in their own home. The cats and dogs in these homes think I'm really giving a lesson to them. Sometimes the pet cat or dog will hop into my lap to watch the piano lesson. Children love having their favorite animals join in.

I have already mentioned my great neighbors in Provincetown. My neighbor Jeannie had two Siamese cats. They came over to visit often. They loved sitting on the lid and watching the hammers move. They would chatter as Siamese cats tend to do and sit on the piano bench to keep me company as I practiced. I even played their favorite song - *Memory* from the Broadway Musical *Cats*. Jeannie's husband Bob was worried that the cats were bothering me. I told him that they weren't a bother at all, and I loved it when they came to visit while I practiced. At the time we had a horrible lady who was on the condo board. You all know the type of person I'm referring to - extremely disagreeable. When she appeared the cats started hissing. It was quite a scene. Animals really can tell who the good guys are.

This brings me to a commentary by Sir Donald Francis Tovey. He was a British piano professor and scholar who wrote witty and astute essays on Beethoven Sonatas. When he got to Sonata 22 he wrote: "(this Sonata) is childlike, or even dog-like, and those who best understand children and dogs have the best chance of enjoying an adequate reading of this music."

Michael Caine's book *Acting in Film*

In his book *Acting in Film,* Michael Caine remarks, "I can't say it enough: one of the most important things an actor can do in a motion picture is to listen and react as freshly as if it were for the first time."

That's exactly the advice for musicians as well. You must listen with all your attention, focus, and react. You react to what you just heard, and as you play envision what comes next. Your abilities of concentration must be at their peak as you are doing three things simultaneously:

1. React to what you just heard.
2. Listen to what is happening at the moment it is occurring.
3. Envision what will come next.

As you create on the spur of the moment you may surprise yourself. React to the surprise and wonder of the music.

Remember our discussion of microphones? I said you shouldn't over-play or over-accent. The microphones don't like it. There is a parallel in film acting. Michael Caine devotes many pages to how the camera (just like the microphone) takes everything in. It doesn't lie. You don't have to overact for the camera. It captures all the subtleties at once. Many Broadway performers who are used to playing to the balcony in a Broadway theater have trouble learning to tone down their acting for the screen. There is a wonderful story about Jack Lemmon before the camera early in his career as told by Michael Caine. Jack had come to Hollywood via Broadway and his director was the relentless George Cukor.

George: "Cut. Less, Jack less."

And Jack would do the scene again.

George: "Cut. Less, Jack less."

And Jack would do the scene again.

George: "Cut. Less, Jack less."

Jack: "But if I do any less, I'll be doing nothing."

George: "*Now* you've got it!"

How I Memorize Music

People always ask me how I memorize music. I play almost

everything from memory and like most concert pianists, keeping hundreds of thousands of notes in my head is part of my daily routine. Memorizing music is also an important part of the process of making a piece of music your own. Interpreting a piece of music takes a tremendous positive leap forward when your eyes are no longer glued to the music rack. Imagine, for instance, the difference between an actor reading Shakespeare from a book, as opposed to performing it, where the words are totally memorized and integrated into your every thought, mood and action.

There are many types of memory - aural memory, muscle memory, emotional memory, and visual memory - all these play a part in the instant recall necessary to perform from memory. I work on all four in various ways.

Aural memory means I can hear the entire score in my head. I will actually play the right hand of a piece while only hearing the left hand in my mind. Then I will play the left hand alone while hearing the right hand. As I do this, I also visualize the hand I am not playing, with every detail including the proper fingering. If I'm on an airplane, I may run through an entire concert in my mind, during the flight. I will do this while relaxing on the beach as well. I'll hear the music and visualize each note on the keyboard with the proper fingering. These visualization exercises give security.

There were similar visualization studies done with basketball players. Half the basketball players were told to practice shooting baskets from the foul line. The other half were told to sit in the bleachers and simply visualize shooting baskets with their mind. All the students were tested. The students who practiced only using the visualizations shot baskets with more success than the students who did the actual physical practice.

This study shows the power of the mind.

Muscle memory can be very dangerous to rely upon without a back-up. When I talk of muscle memory, I mean the exact physical movements of your fingers and how the muscles and fingers feel as they play the sequence of notes. Muscle memory is dangerous because it can't always be counted on to work. It is like reciting the words to the same prayer over and over where one's mind is disconnected from the meaning of it all. Rote repetition can be deadly to music. It prevents the performer from being engaged in what he is doing. Never practice a passage over and over the same way. Vary your routine. Play different volumes, different rhythms, only portions of the sequence, such as bass and soprano notes, leaving out the middle notes. The point is, blind repetition to improve your muscle memory will not work.

Pianists are always playing on different instruments. That is another danger of relying on muscle memory. Every time we travel to some place new, we have a different piano with a totally different feel, a different piano sound and different hall acoustics. Suppose you are practicing on a piano with a heavy action. By that I mean a piano where there is resistance in the key and it takes extra effort to depress it. Then suddenly you are playing a concert on a piano with a light action - the keys move if you just blow on them. You must quickly adjust your touch. The entire piano feels different.

A hall sounds different when it is full and when it is empty. More of the sound is absorbed by people when a hall is full, causing less reverberation. When you do a concert run through in an empty hall, be prepared for a different sound experience later after your audience arrives. The feel of the piano changes psychologically when the acoustics change, so keys are touched differently in different acoustics. When someone says, "she has a beautiful touch at the piano," what they are really saying is, she has a sensitivity to playing that makes the sound beautiful in many different conditions. When I play in a church with lots of reverberation, I use less pedal and slightly detach the notes so they sound clearer. If I'm playing in a room with a rug, or acoustic tile that soaks up the sound of the piano, I will play with more pedal and connect the notes in a way that helps sustain them for longer periods of time.

Emotional memory concerns the feelings that wash over me as I play. I have emotions that come over me with every note I play - most of the time very specific feelings. Just as you react word by word as someone talks to you, I react note by note as I play music. These emotions are visceral, and if I connect with them as I play, the actual memory of the music comes back to me easily, without struggle, as I connect emotions to notes. I sometimes even "feel" colors associated with individual notes or chords. If I was to be so crude as to give you words that might go with these feelings I might use words like happy, rude, ironic, angry, joyful, peaceful, hateful, sweet, hard, soft, tragic - well of course I could come up with thousands of words. But that would still be inadequate. Music brings up feelings that words by themselves can only approximate. *If words alone could do it, we would have no need for music.* What I feel as I play cannot be described accurately with words.

Visual memory: There are two types of visual memory - a visual memory of the actual page of music and a visual memory of what it looks like for the hands to move over the keyboard. Rubinstein probably had a photographic memory when it came to his visual recall of a page of music. He says his mind could see everything on a page of music including the coffee stains.

Around 1975 he was playing for a special pension fund benefit concert with the New York Philharmonic. Daniel Barenboim was the conductor and Rubinstein asked him if they could go to Patelson's - the famous sheet music store in New York. Rubinstein had left his personal score at his home in Paris. He wanted to find the exact edition of the Brahms *D Minor Piano Concerto* that he left behind in Paris so visually he wouldn't be confused by an edition he wasn't used to. He needed a visual reminder of the score as he had learned it. Rubinstein was almost 90 at this time and he had been playing this concerto since he was 15! (For those of you who are still not sure what I'm talking about, think of all the different editions of Shakespeare's Hamlet that must be available - some with larger type, some with smaller type, darker type, lighter type, some editions with a different word here or there, some with printers' mistakes. It's the same with music. There are many different published editions of the same piece and they all look different on the printed page.) I actually remember if a musical phase is written on the upper left hand corner of a page, or the bottom right hand corner of a page. Studying the same printed score over and over can be helpful as a memory aid.

The visual memory of what the hands look like moving over the keyboard is important. Claudio Arrau talks of practicing his pieces blindfolded. That is an excellent way of gaining confidence with difficult music. I recently played *The Stars and Stripes Forever* in concert. There are so many difficult jumps - sometimes the hand jumps almost a full yard in an eighth of a second - and I practiced the entire piece with my eyes closed the day before the concert, just to gain more security. I will also practice looking at a jump visually. I judge the distance with my eye just before my hand takes off to the new spot, much like aiming a bow and arrow.

You all know what the actor's nightmare is. You end up on stage in front of thousands of people and can't remember a word of your script. We also have the pianist's nightmare and it is just as terrifying. We walk out on stage and can't remember what we are about to play. Memory work is how we prevent the pianist's nightmare.

Chapter Eight

Chopin's Rules

Frédéric Chopin

Chopin had several rules for his students' practice regimen. Here are a few of them.

1. Fingering is everything. It makes sense that knowing exactly what finger you want to use for every note is critical. If the fingering in a score is the original fingering by Liszt or Chopin, it is probably the best. However, many scores have a disclaimer saying "edited and fingered by ..." Many times the person who edited and fingered the score is some unknown fellow in a publishing house who can't really play the piano. I throw out 40% of the fingering I find in most music scores. It is useless. As I get older I get more and more obsessive with fingering. I write it all out in my scores so I won't forget. I'm probably stricter with my younger students about good fingering than anything else. It is the basis for being a professional pianist.

2. *Listen to good singers. From them you will learn the secret of a beautiful tone.* Chopin loved the *bel canto* singers in the operas of Bellini and Donizetti. Bel canto means *beautiful voice*. I always give the example of *I'm Always Chasing Rainbows* - the bel canto tune that Chopin wrote as the middle section of his *Fantasie Impromptu* that later became a Tin Pan Alley hit. Chopin's Nocturnes also tried to capture this style of melody created by Bellini. The legato (smooth) style of the great singers had a decided influence on Chopin's music and his way of playing it.

3. *Always practice on a good piano that is in tune.* Self-explanatory.

4. *The left hand is the conductor, it must not waver or lose ground; do with the right hand what you will and can.* Chopin is talking here of *rubato* which means to rob the time. It is a specific way of playing slightly out of time. Liszt's famous definition of rubato is similar: "Do you see those trees? The wind plays in the leaves, life unfolds and develops beneath them, but the tree remains the same - that is the Chopin Rubato!"

5. *Do not throw your hands in the air for show. That is like catching pigeons.* I really have tried to follow this advice - sometimes without success.

Paul's Rules

I have three rules to add to Chopin's:

1. *Pedal late.* It is better to put the right pedal down (sometimes called the sostenuto pedal or the loud pedal) *after*

the note or chord has sounded. Pedaling after a chord has sounded gives the chord more focus and body. As a student, when playing the Liszt *First Piano Concerto,* I put the pedal down before the first big chord sounded. That is wrong. It makes the sound slightly unfocused because when the pedal is down, all the strings are free to vibrate. I now delay the pedal by a fraction of a second. The sound is better. You can find many passages in music where this idea works.

2. *Only perform music you are in love with.* Never play anything in public that you don't love. Sometimes you may enjoy a piece of music for a while, and then come to realize it is not as good as you once thought. I recorded a piece by Billy Joel called *Nunley's Carousel.* It's a waltz and it does have a certain charm to it. I began playing it in public and found that the music didn't hold up after repeated performances so I stopped playing it in public. If you fall out of love with a piece of music, don't play it for an audience.

3. *Kill your television.* I saw this as a bumper sticker and I adopted it. There is no way to get through the mountains of piano repertoire needed to master the piano and still watch television. What an enormous time killer television is. (The same goes for surfing the web.) For my entire life I have never subscribed to cable television. I am weak - I admit it. I'd become a couch potato in no time if I had access to television. My home on the Cape has no cable and is out 30 miles into the middle of the Atlantic Ocean. There is no television reception. As someone who has filmed programs for television I recognize the irony. When my first television show premiered, I called a friend and told him that he had to throw a party for me on premiere night because I didn't have a working television set.

It's all in the Details

If you are bored with a piece of music, you probably are not looking closely enough at the details. Phrasing is one area where even the most advanced musician can take a closer look. In conversation we always chop up our sentences into small bites to make ourselves intelligible. There is always a slight pause where we take our breath to make the intent clearer. All the carefully placed commas in this book are places where the sentence needs to breathe. These pauses can be infinitesimal, but they are there. In music we also need to breathe. You may think of a phrase as a sentence of music. These phrases (written on the page as slightly curved lines over the groups of notes you wish to phrase) are put in by the composers. Mozart and Haydn may have phrases of just two notes - little sighs. Chopin can have one long phrase that goes on for two lines. The notes in a phrase need to be carefully connected. In between the phrase is where we take a little silence or breath. I remind my students that these composers had to dip their quill pens in their ink pots just to make these little phrase marks. It was a lot of extra work. Often the great composers will phrase in unexpected ways, making phrases go over bar lines or in unexpected groupings. Following the composer's original phrase marks is a good way to invigorate your playing. The writer Anna Quindlen said, "Punctuation is everything." For a composer, "Phrasing is everything." Let your music breathe.

Voice and Piano

Voice is more difficult to teach than piano. One cannot see what is happening inside the throat. Piano teachers can at least see hands, wrists, arms, and elbows, but with voice everything is hidden. Voice teachers and pianists often talk of relaxation and breathing - topics crucial in teaching voice, but important to piano playing as well. I'm going to surprise you now with an observation about piano playing. To play the piano well you must support the diaphragm and spine just as singers do. Many piano teachers ignore this support issue, and if a piano student hunches over, or allows the diaphragm to collapse, the sound also collapses. Collapsing the spine constricts everything - whether you round your shoulders or crouch over the piano. It actually constricts the sound in both singing and instrumental performance. Look at Rubinstein's posture in his videos. Even at age eighty-nine his shoulders were always straight. He never was bent or stooped and hardly ever allowed his head to droop down at the keyboard. He sat at the piano like a king, looking straight ahead.

Brian Lee in the studio.

It's a good idea for pianists to talk to voice teachers about this issue. Chopin always recommended that pianists work with good singers. My go-to guy on this topic is Brian Lee. He is a voice teacher just outside Washington, D.C. He has played flute and viola in symphony orchestras, plays the piano and is an expert voice teacher. Being both a singer and an instrumentalist gives him a unique perspective. His blog at vocalability.com has been cited in music magazines as one of the top 50 singing blogs. Brian writes posts on vocal freedom, breathing, and the art of conveying legato to students. Many of his insights apply to pianists as well as singers.

Pianists as they Get Older

I have a particular affection for pianists who are older. The maturity that comes with older musicians is like an expensive wine - complex and carefully aged. I have in my possession the complete recordings of Rubinstein. They number about 80 CDs and with many works there are several recordings of the same piece. To hear a work he recorded in 1932, recorded again in 1952 and then again in 1964 is to hear a transformation from a great musician to a transcendental one. For him, making music was a metaphysical process. As he got older the music became simpler, more transparent and the sound became even deeper and richer. Max Wilcox was Rubinstein's long time recording engineer at RCA. When Rubinstein made some of his last recordings at age eighty-nine, Wilcox, remarking on this simplicity said, "Rubinstein will end up playing a simple C major scale and reduce us all to tears!"

Claudio Arrau in his eighties also reached that point where the music became deeper and richer. Arrau noted that it was easier to play the piano as he got older. Passages that he used to struggle with now seemed to come with ease. He didn't have to practice as much. The muscles had a wisdom of their own and the work was being done subconsciously. The muscles in the hands and arms automatically knew what to do without conscious thought.

I have a video of Mieczyslaw Horzowski playing at Carnegie Hall. He is almost one-hundred years old and his playing is divine. At that age the musician becomes magician. It seems these old men had in their possession a secret elixir. That magic elixir was called "distilled essence of music."

The older pianists had another trait. They moved very little at the keyboard. Watch videos of Horowitz or Rubinstein. They don't move that much. Sometimes, you can't really tell that they are doing anything. They are quiet at the keyboard. They don't make faces. They don't stamp their feet. They don't hum or make noises. They sit up straight and don't hunch over the keyboard so their playing has a nobility and majesty to it. They don't sway back and forth. They don't even look down at their hands very much. They look straight ahead and their hands effortlessly float over the keyboard. I put both Luiz de Moura Castro and Nigel Coxe in the realm of those pianists, as you may have noticed, from the descriptions of them in this book.

One more thought on pianists and conductors: almost all the great pianists and conductors I have mentioned lived into their 90s and 100s. Stokowski lived to 95 and had a recording contract with RCA that extended to the age of 105. Irving Berlin lived to 101. Serkin, Rubinstein, Horowitz, Arrau, Shura Cherkassy, Nigel Coxe and Luiz de Moura Castro all played some of the best concerts of their careers in their 70s and 80s. I'm hoping to do the same.

A Rachmaninoff CD

In the late 1980s, I was thrilled to play concerts with cellist Christopher Pegis. He came from a family of string players. As I write this he has a brother with the Chicago Symphony and another brother with the Sarasota Symphony. Chris is the founder and director of the Amici Chamber Players. We played a good deal of the piano and cello literature together and had even made a recording of the great Rachmaninoff *Sonata for Cello and Piano*. This piece is a favorite of mine and everyone just falls in love with the tender, sentimental slow movement of this masterpiece.

As I have mentioned many times, the Russian cellist Raya Garbousova was friends with all her Russian compatriots including Rostropovich, Horowitz and Rachmaninoff. Isaac Stern who managed to save Carnegie Hall from demolition in the late 70s put together a big birthday bash for the much beloved musical landmark. Garbousova was in the hall for this historic event, and wouldn't you know, the featured soprano for the evening suddenly became ill. Unexpectedly, to the surprise and delight of everyone, Horowitz and Rostropovich walked together, unannounced onto the stage of Carnegie Hall. You could feel the electricity of this historic moment. What would they play? The slow movement of the Rachmaninoff *Sonata for Cello and Piano*. As one reviewer put it, two old Russian émigrés crammed full of memories singing a hymn to mother Russia. Garbousova told me there wasn't a dry eye in the house. Of course I bought the recording and played it over and over. Columbia Masterworks wanted Horowitz and Rostropovich to record all 4 movements of the sonata complete, but Horowitz with his difficult temperament backed out at the last minute.

Many of us still dream of what could have been, had these two legends recorded this unique work in its entirety.

Now we come to my personal connection to this great Sonata. Garbousova had told me about cuts to the last movement of the sonata, which Rachmaninoff himself had personally authorized to her. The piece is big - over a half hour long. Chris and I liked Rachmaninoff's idea for the cuts. I also heard Madame Garbousova play the Sonata with my teacher Raymond Hanson. Then Chris Pegis asked if I would record it with him. Chris has lots of courage in his cello playing and we attacked this piece with vigor. We played it for David Finckel, the Grammy winning cellist with the Emerson String Quartet, as well as for Luiz de Moura Castro. I will never forget Luiz's wonderful suggestion to hold the pedal down and not change it for huge segments. He showed me that if you play the notes with enough finesse, you don't need to change the pedal so often and you can let the notes mingle in a way that makes the music soar and resound with an even more beautiful mix of the harmonies. We made a recording at the Hartt School and the school entered it in a competition. Our recording of the Rachmaninoff Sonata won the *McGraw Hill Young Artists Showcase Award*. It was broadcast on WQXR in New York with Robert Sherman as host. The radio station actually sent me a copy of the broadcast where it sat upon my shelf for over 20 years. For some reason I forgot about the recording. Fast forward to 2012. I was working on a new CD project with my recording engineer. I told him I had an old air tape from WQXR in New York that I never had even listened to. I asked him to make a digital transfer of the tape to see if it was any good. My recording engineer and I were blown away by how good the recording was. I just fell in love again with Chris Pegis' fabulous cello playing. I called Chris and I asked if he had the original master. He told me his master had deteriorated in the Florida heat and humidity. I asked my recording engineer if he could restore the recording for commercial release from my WQXR air tape. Recording technology is so good now that a recording such as the one we made in 1988 can be restored to sound like it was recorded yesterday. Chris listened to the remastered recording and authorized its release. I had recorded a good deal of Rachmaninoff solo piano music previously so that is how I managed to release *A Rachmaninoff Album* which included the recording of my favorite cello sonata with Chris Pegis.

I'll add one more Raya Garbousova story. Besides Rachmaninoff, she knew many more 20th century icons. She was also one of the great beauties of her day, and there is a story from her early years regarding that. She took on a five-dollar wager at a party to kiss Toscanini, who was sitting at the table next to hers. The maestro was delighted to be approached by such a beautiful young girl and offered the other cheek. Encouraged by his enthusiasm Raya kissed him on both cheeks with the excuse that she could now claim ten dollars.

Playing *Rhapsody in Blue* at Aeolian Hall in New York

A certain amount of luck led to the creation of *Rhapsody in Blue*. The luck (as it often did) started with Gershwin playing the piano at a party - this was a Christmas party in 1923. Gershwin loved to play the piano for friends at parties. Paul Whiteman, the big band leader, went up to Gershwin as he was entertaining and mentioned that he'd like Gershwin to write something for his orchestra. Gershwin said he'd do it - and then he forgot about it. At the time, he was putting the finishing touches on a show called *Sweet Little Devil*. The show was being tried out in Boston. In January of 1924 Gershwin was going back and forth between New York and Boston to oversee the opening of his new show. At the beginning of January, George's brother Ira, who was always watching for interesting items in the newspapers, saw a very interesting article in the *New York Herald Tribune*. This article said that George Gershwin was at work on a brand new piano concerto, to be premiered by the Paul Whiteman Orchestra at Aeolian Hall, on Lincoln's Birthday. Lincoln's Birthday was five weeks away. No one could possibly write a full length piano concerto in five weeks. Gershwin thought he could perhaps do a shorter one movement work. He got on the train to Boston with his sketch books. Every good composer has sketch books. You think of a good tune and write it down in the sketch book. Gershwin found some ideas he liked and started writing out *Rhapsody in Blue* page by page on the train to Boston.

In 1931 Gershwin reminisced to his first biographer, Isaac Goldberg about his creation: "It was on the train, with its steely rhythms, its rattle-ty bang, that is so often so stimulating to a composer - I frequently hear music in the very heart of the noise... And there I suddenly heard, and even saw on paper - the complete construction of the *Rhapsody*, from beginning to end. No new themes came to me, but I worked on the thematic material already in my mind and tried to conceive the composition as a whole. I heard it as a sort of musical kaleido-scope of America, of our vast melting pot, of our unduplicated national pep, of our metropolitan madness. By the time I reached Boston I had a definite plot of the piece."

Everyone was nervous about the premiere of *Rhapsody in Blue* because there was so little time for rehearsal. Besides that, many celebrities would be in attendance for the premiere including Sergei Rachmaninoff and John Phillip Sousa. The concert was a huge success and *Rhapsody in Blue* became one of the most successful concert works ever written by an American composer.

I had no idea that the Aeolian building still exists, but it does. It is on 42nd street not far from Times Square. The silver art deco lettering still exists at the front of the building but the original auditorium no longer does. The city of New York now owns the building and a new, more intimate hall was built on this landmark site. In October 2008, I was invited to perform *Rhapsody in Blue* at inauguration ceremonies for this new hall, on the very site where Gershwin first performed his legendary masterpiece. (Rachmaninoff, Paderewski and Busoni also performed on this site.) As I stood in the wings on the night of that concert, just before my entrance onto this historic space, I was overcome with the emotional connection to the giants of music, present in spirit, on this hallowed ground.

Giving a Lecture at Trinity College

I recently gave a lecture for the music department at Trinity College in Hartford. I mentioned Arthur Rubinstein and Fred Astaire to the students. None of them had heard of these 20th century icons. I suppose they could be forgiven. Astaire and Rubinstein had already been dead for several years before these students were even born. The following week I arrived with DVDs of Rubinstein and Astaire and showed excerpts. The sheer elegance and power of these artists left the students gasping. They had never seen or heard anything like that before. I was particularly anxious to make a point with the Astaire videos -

the interconnection of the arts at all levels. The grace and elegance of Astaire's movements can easily be translated to piano practicing. When we watch Astaire we see movements that have been practiced thousands of times until they become subconscious.

Astaire's perfectionism allowed him to become comfortable in these motions. Astaire's movements look so natural. The physical motions and gestures become more expressive, even at the smallest level. That is exactly what happens in piano playing.

Fred Astaire was detail oriented. He would often work on a number for three to five weeks before he went before the camera to actually shoot it. When Debbie Reynolds was working on *Singing in the Rain*, Gene Kelly apparently insulted her for her lack of dance experience. Fred Astaire found Reynolds crying under a piano. He took her to his studio and showed her his work methods. He was very clear that the polish of his routines came from constant work and revision. It didn't come naturally, even to him. I often watch Fred Astaire to get inspiration for my work at the piano.

My 2012 Season

The 2012 season was a big one for me. We celebrated Luiz's 70th birthday with three festive days and nights of concerts and dinners. I also gave concerts throughout the country, released a new DVD, three new CDs, and wrote this book. I'm calling 2012 another "Champagne Year." Here below is a short speech I gave at the University of Hartford helping to celebrate Luiz's big year too:

Luiz de Moura Castro 35th Year at Hartt and 70th Birthday

Celebration

Millard Auditorium, The Hartt School, University of Hartford.

What a wonderful celebration. I loved Tom Mastrianni's referral to Liszt, spirituality and transfiguration, and Luiz's strong connection to these principles as a teacher, performer and mentor. Thank you Tom for that. Now I'd like to take it a step further. There is a saying among people who teach spiritual practice that, "when the pupil is ready the master will appear." It has been a common theme throughout these concerts that Luiz, somehow magically, appears at the time he is needed. I don't know how you do it Luiz, but with this uncanny knack, you suddenly appear at the right place and transform people and situations at just the right moment. Jonathan Moyer, Martha Summa, and Laura Garritson, all wonderful performers here today, said as much. I have seen it many times myself.

I was so happy to hear that a student of Laura's mom will be studying with Luiz this year. One of my students will also study with Luiz starting this year. "When the pupil is ready, the master will appear." And so the magic continues for another generation.

You know, I was lucky to actually witness the day Luiz walked through the halls of this school for the very first time. There must have been about 40 piano majors here and Luiz gave lessons to everyone that day. In little groups we would hover around the pianos in Raymond Hanson's studio and watch Luiz make everyone play better. He had that magic ability from the first day he arrived and we all witnessed it. Then, after a full day of teaching, Luiz walked into this very hall and launched into a heroic performance of the Liszt *Sonata*. I sat at the back of the hall next to Raymond Hanson, and at the end of the concert Ray whispered to me "You know, no one can really keep up a pace like that for very long." Well, Luiz has managed to keep up that incredible pace for the last 35 years. At this moment, I couldn't be prouder of my school for having a master like my teacher and friend Luiz de Moura Castro.

Two piano recital with Luiz de Moura Castro. First Church Springfield, MA. (Photo courtesy Charlie Sanden)

Finale

It's time to draw the curtain. Thank-you to all my readers for allowing me to connect with you through this book. It has been an honor. I look forward to the possibility of playing the piano for you in person. In fact, I can't wait to play the piano for you.

What have I learned from jotting down all these memories? First of all, time has passed more quickly than I realized. It seems like only last month I was a song *plugger* in the downtown Hartford hotels. Secondly, I am so indebted to my teachers. I would not have succeeded without their immense generosity of time and talent. Finally, music is not about fame, money or success. It is about enriching and deepening our lives. How lucky we are to have music, which gives us the means to express the inexpressible.

Paul Bisaccia

December 2012
Provincetown, Massachusetts.

A SUGGESTED CREATIVE READING LIST

Sometimes there are books you can't put down because they are so well written. Here are some suggestions for books that musicians - or anyone who aspires to creativity - should read. Most of them have already been referenced in these pages. They are all eye-openers.

Franz Liszt by Alan Walker, in 3 volumes (Truly one of the greatest biographies ever written and winner of too many awards to even mention.)

The Great Pianists by Harold C. Schonberg (Absorbing prose and fun to read, by the legendary *New York Times* music critic.)

The Great Composers also by Harold C. Schonberg

Acting in Film by Michael Caine (If you are going to appear before the camera, or if you love the art of film, read this book.)

Conversations with Arrau by Joseph Horowitz (Required reading for concert pianists.)

My Younger Years by Arthur Rubinstein (One of the most significant memoirs of the 20th century.)

The Way of the Wizard by Deepak Chopra (Looking at reality differently.)

The Once and Future King by T.H. White (A re-telling of the

King Arthur legend, but really a look at war and civilization with new eyes.)

Music Study in Germany by Amy Fay (Contains absorbing eye witness account of the celebrated Liszt Masterclasses.)

Outliers by Malcolm Gladwell (How people become successful in what they do.)

On Writing by Stephen King (The best discussion on the craft of writing. It can easily be applied to many artistic endeavors.)

Finishing the Hat by Stephen Sondheim (A look into the mind of that creative genius.)

Schumann - The Inner Voices of a Musical Genius by Peter Ostwald (Winner of the ASCAP-Deems Taylor Award for excellence in writing on the subject of music.)

Beethoven - The Music and the Life by Lewis Lockwood (A Pulitzer Prize finalist.)

The Gershwins and Me by Michael Feinstein (The best book about the Gershwins I've ever read.)

BISACCIA TELEVISION PROGRAMS

Gershwin by Bisaccia

Paul Bisaccia and the Great American Piano

Chopin by Bisaccia

Released on DVD:

Bisaccia on Television!

Filmed at Steinway Hall in New York City and venues throughout New England, here's two hours of great piano performances from Paul Bisaccia's PBS television shows. The music includes Chopin, Liszt, Prokofieff, Rachmaninoff and "Great American Piano" composers Gershwin, Joplin, Gottschalk, Eubie Blake and Sousa. Mr. Bisaccia gives fascinating commentary and the world premiere of a major piano work by nineteenth century composer Dudley Buck. He also plays the music of Chopin on a rare 1896 Rosewood Steinway and shares remembrances of Horowitz and Rubinstein.

BISACCIA DISCOGRAPHY

These recordings are available on CD Baby and Amazon as well as through the iTunes and Spotify apps.

73 composers, 320 works
Sorted by composer
Album title in *italics*

Adolphe Adam
O Holy Night, *Classic Christmas / Jazz Christmas*

Isaac Albeniz
Sevilla, *Moonlight Sonata*
Tango, *Moonlight Sonata*
Segudillas, *Moonlight Sonata*

Leroy Anderson
Sleigh Ride, *Classic Christmas / Jazz Christmas*

Harold Arlen
Over the Rainbow, (classical version) *I Love a Piano*
Over the Rainbow, (jazz version) *I Love a Piano*

J.S. Bach
Jesu Joy of Man's Desiring, *Classic Christmas / Jazz Christmas*
Prelude in C, W.T.C. Book 1, *Clair de Lune*
Toccata and Fugue in D minor, (arr. Busoni) *Masterworks*

Samuel Barber
Blues from "Excursions," *An American in Paris - Great American Composers*

Ludwig van Beethoven
Für Elise, *Moonlight Sonata*
Sonata "Pathetique" in C minor, Op. 13, *Clair de Lune*
Sonata "Moonlight" in C-sharp minor, Op. 27 no. 2, *Moonlight Sonata*
Sonata "Appassionata" in F minor, Op. 57, *Appassionata*

Irving Berlin
Alexander's Ragtime Band, *The Great American Piano Revisited*
Everybody's Doin' it Now (with John Thomas) *Four Hands, Two Guys, One Piano!*
I Love a Piano, *I Love a Piano*
Puttin' on the Ritz, *Stars and Stripes Forever - The Great American Piano*
When the Midnight Choo Choo Leaves for Alabam (with John Thomas) *Four Hands, Two Guys, One Piano!*

Felix Bernard
Winter Wonderland, *Classic Christmas / Jazz Christmas*

Leonard Bernstein
Overture to Candide, An *American in Paris - Great American Composers*

Eubie Blake
Troublesome Ivories, *The Great American Piano Revisited*
The Chevy Chase, *The Great American Piano Revisited*
Tricky Fingers, *The Great American Piano Revisited*

Euday L. Bowman
Twelfth Street Rag, *Stars and Stripes Forever - The Great American Piano*

Johannes Brahms
Lullaby (Wiegenlied) op. 49, no. 4, *Ragtime Lullabies*
Variations on a Theme of Paganini, *Mussorgsky, Brahms, Liszt*
- Book 1 complete
- Book 2 complete

Dave Brubeck
Blue Rondo a la Turk, *An American in Paris -Great American Composers*

Dudley Buck
Introduction and Rondo Brillante Op. 7, *The Great American Piano Revisited*

Zez Confrey
Dizzy Fingers, *Stars and Stripes Forever- The Great American Piano*
Kitten on the Keys, *Stars and Stripes Forever- The Great American Piano*
Novellette, *I Love a Piano*

Aaron Copland
Hoedown (from Rodeo) *An American in Paris - Great American Composers*

Frederic Chopin
Ballade No. 1 in G minor, Op. 23, *Chopin*
Ballade No. 3 in A-flat major, Op. 47, *Clair de Lune*
Etude in E major, Op. 10 no. 3, *Moonlight Sonata*
Etude in C minor "Revolutionary" Op. 10 no. 12, *Moonlight Sonata*
Etude in A-flat major, Op. 25 no. 1, *Moonlight Sonata*
Fantasie-Impromptu in C-sharp minor, Op. 66, *Chopin*

Mazurka in D major, Op. 33 No. 2, *Masterworks*
Nocturne in E-flat major, Op. 9 no.. 2, *Chopin*
Nocturne n D-flat major, Op. 27 no. 2, *Masterworks*
Prelude G major, Op. 28 no. 3, *Chopin*
Prelude A major, Op. 28 no. 7, *Chopin*
Prelude B minor, Op. 28 no. 6, *Chopin*
Prelude E major, Op. 28 no. 9,*Chopin*
Prelude D-flat major "Raindrop" Op. 28 no. 15, *Chopin*
Prelude F-sharp major, Op. 28 no. 13, *Appassionata*
Prelude C minor, Op. 28 no. 20, *Chopin*
Prelude D minor, Op. 28 no. 24, *Appassionata*
Polonaise in A major, Op. 40 no. 1 "Military" *Chopin*
Polonaise in F-sharp minor, Op. 44, *Masterworks*
Polonaise in A-flat major, Op. 53 "Heroic" *Chopin*
Scherzo no. 1 in B minor, Op. 20, *Masterworks*
Scherzo no. 2 in B-Flat minor, Op. 31, *Appassionata*
Sonata no. 2, Op. 35 "Funeral March" *Chopin*
Waltz Op. 18 in E-Flat, *Chopin*
Waltz in A-flat major, Op. 34 no. 1, *Masterworks*
Waltz in A minor, Op. 34 no. 2, *Waltzes Rare and Familiar*
Waltz in D-flat, Op. 64 no. 1 "Minute" *Blue Danube - Waltzes Rare and Familiar*
Waltz in C-sharp minor, Op. 64 no.2, *Blue Danube - Waltzes Rare and Familiar*
Waltz in E minor, Op. posth., *Blue Danube - Waltzes Rare and Familiar*
Waltz in A-flat major "L'Adieu" Op. 69 no. 1, *Appassionata*

Claude Debussy
Arabesque no. 1, *Appassionata*
Clair de Lune, *Clair de Lune*

Golliwog's Cakewalk, *Ragtime Lullabies*
Jimbo's Lullaby, *Ragtime Lullabies*
Prelude General, Lavine eccentric, *I Love a Piano*
Prelude Maid with the Flaxen Hair, *I Love a Piano*
Prelude Minstrels, *I Love a Piano*
Prelude from "Pour le Piano," *I Love a Piano*
Valse - La plus que lente, *I Love a Piano*

Paul Desmond
Take Five, *Stars and Stripes Forever - The Great American Piano*

Danny Elfman
The Simpsons Theme, *The Great American Piano Revisited*

Duke Ellington
It Don't Mean a Thing if it Ain't Got That Swing, *Stars and Stripes Forever - The Great American Piano*

Manuel de Falla
Ritual Fire Dance, *Moonlight Sonata*

César Franck
Sonata for Violin and Piano, *Franck, Gershwin, Meyer, Chopin*
With Jason Meyer, violinist

Jack Fina
Bumble Boogie, *The Great American Piano Revisited*

Stephen Foster
*Jeanie with the Light Brown Hair, *The Great American Piano Revisited*
My Old Kentucky Home, *An American in Paris - Great American Composers*

Swanee River, *The Great American Piano Revisited*
Theme and Variations on Old Black Joe (arr.Snelling) *The Great American Piano Revisited*
Recording with vocalist David Giardina

Joe Garland
In the Mood, *I Love a Piano*

Erroll Garner
Misty, *I Love a Piano*

George Gershwin
An American in Paris (piano transcription by William Daly arr. Bisaccia) *An American in Paris - Great American Composers*
*Blah Blah Blah, *Simply Gershwin*
Clap Yo' Hands, *Rhapsody in Blue - Gershwin's Complete Solo Piano Music*
Clap Yo' Hands, *Stars and Stripes Forever - The Great American Piano*
Do It Again, *Rhapsody in Blue - Gershwin's Complete Solo Piano Music*
*Do It Again, *Simply Gershwin*
Do - Do - Do, *Rhapsody in Blue - Gershwin's Complete Solo Piano Music*
*Do Do Do, *Simply Gershwin*
Fascinating Rhythm, *Rhapsody in Blue - Gershwin's Complete Solo Piano Music*
Fascinating Rhythm, *Simply Gershwin*
Fascinating Rhythm, *Stars and Stripes Forever - The Great American Piano*
For Lily Pons, *The Great American Piano Revisited*
Funny Face, *An American in Paris - Great American Composers*

Preludes, *Rhapsody in Blue - Gershwin's Complete Solo Piano Music*
- I Allegro ben ritmato e deciso
- II Andante con moto
- III Allegro ben ritmato e deciso
Prelude, January, *Ragtime Lullabies*
Prelude, Rubato, *Ragtime Lullabies*
Prelude, Sleepless Night, *Ragtime Lullabies*
Prelude Novelette in Fourths, *Ragtime Lullabies*
Promenade, *Rhapsody in Blue - Gershwin's Complete Solo Piano Music*
Ragging the Traumerei, *The Great American Piano Revisited*
The Real American Folk Song is a Rag, *Ragtime Lullabies*
*The Real American Folk Song is a Rag, *Simply Gershwin*
Rhapsody In Blue, *Rhapsody in Blue - Gershwin's Complete Solo Piano Music*
Rialto Ripples Rag, *Rhapsody in Blue - Gershwin's Complete Solo Piano Music*
Rialto Ripples Rag, *Ragtime Lullabies*
Rialto Ripples Rag, *Simply Gershwin*
Someone to Watch Over Me, *Stars and Stripes Forever - The Great American Piano*
That Certain Feeling, *Rhapsody in Blue Gershwin's Complete Solo Piano Music*
**They Can't Take That Away From Me, *The Great American Piano Revisited*
*They Can't Take That Away From Me, *Simply Gershwin*
Three-Quarter Blues, *Rhapsody in Blue - Gershwin's Complete Solo Piano Music*
*Treat Me Rough, *Simply Gershwin*
Two Waltzes In C, *Rhapsody in Blue - Gershwin's Complete Solo*

Piano Music

Somebody Loves Me, *Rhapsody in Blue - Gershwin's Complete Solo Piano Music*

*Someone to Watch Over Me, *Simply Gershwin*

Strike Up The Band, *Rhapsody in Blue - Gershwin's Complete Solo Piano Music*

*Strike Up the Band, *Simply Gershwin*

Summertime, *Ragtime Lullabies*

*Summertime, *Simply Gershwin*

Swanee, *Rhapsody in Blue - Gershwin's Complete Solo Piano Music*

*Swanee, *Simply Gershwin*

Swanee, *Stars and Stripes Forever - The Great American Piano*

Sweet And Low Down, *Rhapsody in Blue - Gershwin's Complete Solo Piano Music*

'S Wonderful, *Rhapsody in Blue - Gershwin's Complete Solo Piano Music*

*'S Wonderful, *Simply Gershwin*

'S Wonderful/Funny Face, *An American in Paris - Great American Composers*

Who Cares, *Rhapsody in Blue - Gershwin's Complete Solo Piano Music*

* *recording with vocalist Diane Penning*
***recording with vocalist David Giardina*

Philip Glass

Escape! from "The Hours," *Appassionata*
Morning Passages from "The Hours," *Clair de Lune*

Louis Moreau Gottschalk

The Banjo, *Stars and Stripes Forever - The Great American Piano*

Columbia - Caprice Americaine, *An American in Paris - Great American Composers*

Grand Scherzo, *The Great American Piano Revisited*

Grand Tarantelle Op. Posth. 67 (with John Thomas), *Four Hands, Two Guys, One Piano!*

Le Bananier, *An American in Paris - Great American Composers*

Ojos Criollos Op. 37 (with John Thomas), *Four Hands, Two Guys, One Piano!*

Radieuse - Grande valse de concert Op. 27 (with John Thomas), *Four Hands, Two Guys, One Piano!*

Tournament Galop, *The Great American Piano Revisited*

Union - Paraphrase on the National Airs Star Spangled Banner, Yankee Doodle and Hail Columbia, *Stars and Stripes Forever - The Great American Piano*

Franz Gruber
Silent Night, *Classic Christmas / Jazz Christmas*

Vince Guaraldi
Linus and Lucy, *Stars and Stripes Forever - The Great American Piano*

Franz Joseph Haydn
Sonata in D Hob. 16/37, *Masterworks*

Marvin Hamlisch
A Chorus Line, *I Love a Piano*
- One
- What I Did for Love

Benjamin Hanby
Up on the Housetop, *Classic Christmas / Jazz Christmas*

George F. Handel
Joy To The World, *Classic Christmas / Jazz Christmas*

Christopher Haynes
Carrol, *Classic Christmas / Jazz Christmas*
Prelude-Contemplation, *Clair de Lune*

Josef Hofmann (arr.)
The Star Spangled Banner, *The Great American Piano Revisited*

Billy Joel
Goodnight My Angel (Lullaby) *Ragtime Lullabies*
New York State of Mind, *The Great American Piano Revisited*
Prelude, *Stars and Stripes Forever -The Great American Piano*
Root Beer Rag, *Ragtime Lullabies*
Waltz #1 "Nunley's Carousel," *An American in Paris - Great American Composers*

Scott Joplin
Bethena - Concert Waltz, *An American in Paris - Great American Composers*
The Cascades, *Ragtime Lullabies*
The Easy Winners, *Ragtime Lullabies*
The Entertainer, *Ragtime Lullabies*
Gladiolus Rag, *The Great American Piano Revisited*
Heliotrope Bouquet, *I Love a Piano*
Maple Leaf Rag, *Ragtime Lullabies*
Pineapple Rag, *Stars and Stripes Forever - The Great American Piano*
Pineapple Rag, *Ragtime Lullabies*
Solace, *Ragtime Lullabies*

Stop Time (with John Thomas) *Four Hands, Two Guys, One Piano!*

Aram Khachaturian
Andantino, *Appassionata*

Ernesto Lecuona
Andalucia, *Clair de Lune*
La Comparsa, *Clair de Lune*
Malaguena, *Clair de Lune*

M. Leontovich
Carol of the Bells, *Classic Christmas / Jazz Christmas*

Franz Liszt
Album Leaf in the Form of a Waltz, *Blue Danube - Waltzes Rare and Familiar*
Concerto no. 1 in E-flat major, *YouTube film clip*
Consolation no. 2 in E major, *Masterworks*
Consolation no. 3 in D-flat major, *Appassionata*
Consolation no. 4 in D-flat major, *A Rachmaninoff Album* (bonus track)
Christmas Tree Suite, *Classic Christmas / Jazz Christmas*
- Old Christmas Song
- The Shepherd's at the Manger (In dulci jubilo)
- Adeste Fidelis as March of the Three Kings
- Scherzoso - Merry Making Upon Lighting the Tree
- Old Provençal Christmas Song
- Slumber Song
Czárdás Obstiné, *Moonlight Sonata*
En Reve, *Masterworks*
Etude in D-Flat "Un Sospiro" *Moonlight Sonata*

Funérailles, *Moonlight Sonata*
Liebestraum no. 3, *Moonlight Sonata*
Mephisto Waltz no. 1, *Blue Danube - Waltzes Rare and Familiar*
Soirees de Vienne: Valse Caprice no. 6 (after Schubert),
Masterworks
Vallée d'Obermann, *Mussorgsky Brahms Liszt*
Valse - Impromptu, *Blue Danube - Waltzes Rare and Familiar*
Valse Oubliée no. 1, *Blue Danube - Waltzes Rare and Familiar*
Valse Oubliée no. 2, *Blue Danube - Waltzes Rare and Familiar*
Valse Oubliée no. 3, *Blue Danube - Waltzes Rare and Familiar*
Valse Oubliée no. 4, *Blue Danube - Waltzes Rare and Familiar*
Waltz from Faust Concert Paraphrase (Gounod) *Blue Danube -
Waltzes Rare and Familiar*

George Lyons and Bob Yosco
Spaghetti Rag, *Ragtime Lullabies*

Henry Mancini
Baby Elephant Walk, *Stars and Stripes Forever - The Great
American Piano*
The Pink Panther, *Stars and Stripes Forever - The Great
American Piano*

Felix Mendelssohn
Rondo Capriccioso Op. 14, *Masterworks*

Jason Meyer
Odessa, *Franck, Gershwin, Meyer, Chopin*

Wolfgang Amadeus Mozart
Rondo a la Turk, *Clair de Lune*

Modeste Mussorgsky
Pictures at an Exhibition, *Mussorgsky, Brahms, Liszt*
Hopak, *Appassionata*

Peter Nero
Scratch My Bach, *Stars and Stripes Forever - The Great American Piano*

Johann Pachelbel
Canon in D, *Clair de Lune*

Ignance J. Paderewski
Melody in B, *I Love a Piano*
Minuet in G, *I Love a Piano*

James Pierpont
Jingle Bells (ragtime version) *Classic Christmas / Jazz Christmas*
Jingle Bells (in homage to Ella) *Classic Christmas / Jazz Christmas*

Sergei Prokofiev
March from "The Love for Three Oranges," *Appassionata*
Romeo and Juliet, *Appassionata*
- The Young Juliet Op. 75 no. 6
- The Montagues and Capulets Op. 75 no. 4

Sergei Rachmaninoff
Etude-Tableaux in C major Op. 33 no. 2, *Moonlight Sonata*
Etude-Tableaux in C major Op. 33 no. 2, *A Rachmaninoff Album*
Flight of the Bumblebee, *The Great American Piano Revisited*
Flight of the Bumblebee, *A Rachmaninoff Album*
Prelude in C-sharp minor Op. 2 no. 3, *Moonlight Sonata*

Prelude in C-sharp minor Op. 2 no. 3, *A Rachmaninoff Album*
Prelude in E-flat major Op. 23 no. 6, *Appassionata*
Prelude in E-flat major Op. 23 no. 6, *A Rachmaninoff Album*
Prelude in D minor Op. 23 no. 3, *Appassionata*
Prelude in D minor Op. 23 no. 3, *A Rachmaninoff Album*
Prelude in G minor Op. 23 no. 5, *Moonlight Sonata*
Prelude in G minor Op. 23 no. 5, *A Rachmaninoff Album*
Hopak, *Appassionata*
Hopak, *A Rachmaninoff Album*
*Sonata for Cello and Piano Op. 19 in G minor, *A Rachmaninoff Album*
* *with cellist Christopher Pegis*

Maurice Ravel
Le Tombeau de Couperin, *Clair de Lune*
- Prelude
- Rigaudon

John Reading
O Come All Ye Faithful (Adeste Fideles) *Classic Christmas / Jazz Christmas*
O Come All Ye Faithful (Adeste Fideles) arr. Franz Liszt, *Classic Christmas / Jazz Christmas*

N. Rimsky-Korsakoff/ arr.Rachmaninoff
Flight of the Bumblebee, *The Great American Piano Revisited*

Richard Rodgers
The Carousel Waltz, *An American in Paris - Great American Composers*

Frederic Rzewski
Winnsboro Cotton Mill Blues, *Stars and Stripes Forever - The Great American Piano*

Eric Satie
Gymnopedies no. 1, *I Love a Piano*
Je te veux, *I Love a Piano*
Le Piccadilly, *I Love a Piano*

Domenico Scarlatti
Sonata in E major, L. 23, *Clair de Lune*
Sonata in G major, L. 349, *Clair de Lune*

Tom Schuttenhelm
Traces of a Certainty, *Stars and Stripes Forever - The Great American Piano*
I Moderately Fast
II With fluency
III With irony

Franz Schubert
Soirées de Vienne: Valse Caprice no. 6 (arr. Liszt) *Masterworks*

Robert Schumann
Novellette in F major Op. 21 no. 1, *I Love a Piano*
Traumerei from Scenes From Childhood, *The Great American Piano Revisited*

Stephen Sondheim
Night Waltz from "A Little Night Music," *An American in Paris - Great American Composers*
Send in the Clowns, *Ragtime Lullabies*

John Phillip Sousa arr. Bisaccia
Semper Fidelis March, *The Great American Piano Revisited*
The Stars and Stripes Forever, *Stars and Stripes Forever - The Great American Piano*
Washington Post March, *An American in Paris - Great American Composers*

Robert Edward Smith
Sicilienne, *Clair de Lune*

Peter I. Tchaikovsky
The Nutcracker Suite, *Classic Christmas / Jazz Christmas*
- March
- Dance of the Sugar Plum Fairies
- Russian Dance
- Dance of the Reed Flutes
- Waltz of the Flowers
The Seasons
- November, Sleigh Ride, *Classic Christmas / Jazz Christmas*
- December, Christmas Waltz, *Classic Christmas / Jazz Christmas*

John Thomas
Dirty Rag, *The Great American Piano Revisited*
Theme and Variations on Amazing Grace, *The Great American Piano Revisited*

Mel Tormé
The Christmas Song (Chestnuts Roasting on an Open Fire)
Classic Christmas / Jazz Christmas

Traditional
Frankie and Johnny, *I Love a Piano*
We Wish You a Merry Christmas, *Classic Christmas / Jazz Christmas*
Deck the Halls, *Classic Christmas / Jazz Christmas*
Away in a Manger, *Classic Christmas / Jazz Christmas*

Fats Waller
Handful of Keys, *I Love a Piano*
Ain't Misbehavin', *I Love a Piano*
Keepin' Out of Mischief Now, *I Love a Piano*

Louis Weber/Paul Bisaccia
Theme and Variations on Battle Hymn of the Republic, *The Great American Piano Revisited*

Andrew Lloyd Webber
Memory (from Cats) *Ragtime Lullabies*
*Think of Me (from Phantom of the Opera) bonus track, *Simply Gershwin*
* *with vocalist Diane Penning*

Richard S. Willis
It Came Upon a Midnight Clear, *Classic Christmas / Jazz Christmas*

ABOUT THE AUTHOR

Paul Bisaccia made his European debut in Romania at age 17 and has performed concerts on four continents. He graduated summa cum laude and first in his class from the Hartt School. His vast repertoire includes the great piano classics and he was the first artist to record the complete solo piano music of Gershwin. His PBS television show *Gershwin by Bisaccia* has been seen by millions and was dubbed into Mandarin Chinese for broadcast in Asia. Michael Feinstein calls *Paul Bisaccia and the Great American Piano*, his second television show for PBS, "imaginative, fun, well played and totally satisfying." His third television show, *Chopin by Bisaccia* has been included in his newest DVD release *Bisaccia on Television*.

The Hartt School honored Paul with the *Alumnus of the Year Award* and the Governor of Connecticut proclaimed *Paul Bisaccia Day* in the State of Connecticut. PBS celebrated the day with a rebroadcast of his television shows. Bisaccia was also honored to perform *Rhapsody in Blue* in inauguration ceremonies for the new theater on the site of Aeolian Hall in New York, where Gershwin himself first performed his legendary masterpiece.

A prolific and versatile recording artist, Paul has recorded over 300 individual compositions covering a wide range of composers, including huge segments of the music of Chopin and Liszt, all available on amazon.com. Many of his television and film clips can be seen on YouTube.

As a teacher: A respected and successful piano teacher, Paul Bisaccia has always divided his career between performance and teaching. At the Hartt School he pursued a five-year program with a double emphasis on piano performance and music education. His love of both teaching and performing is apparent in his PBS television shows where Paul plays and talks about the music he loves.

Bisaccia has given master classes at Colby College in Maine and has lectured at Trinity College in Hartford, Connecticut. He is currently a piano instructor at Trinity College and also teaches privately on his vintage 1926 Steinway at his studio in the Asylum Hill neighborhood in Hartford. He has been on the jury of several music competitions including the University of Connecticut, the University of Hartford, and the international Simone Belsky Piano Competition.

paulbisaccia.com